A Practical Guide to the Mental Capacity Act 2005

T0385400

A Practical Guide to the Mental Capacity Act 2005

Putting the Principles of the Act Into Practice

Matthew Graham and Jakki Cowley

Foreword by Alex Ruck Keene

Jessica Kingsley *Publishers*
London and Philadelphia

The form for assessing mental capacity on page 77, Table 6.1 on pages 139–40, and the Best-Interests Checklist on pages 144–5 are reproduced with kind permission of the Kent and Medway MCA Local Implementation Network.

First published in 2015
by Jessica Kingsley Publishers
73 Collier Street
London N1 9BE, UK
and
400 Market Street, Suite 400
Philadelphia, PA 19106, USA

www.jkp.com

Copyright © Matthew Graham and Jakki Cowley 2015
Foreword copyright © Alex Ruck Keene 2015

Front cover image source: Shutterstock®.

Library of Congress Cataloging in Publication Data
A CIP catalog record for this book is available from the Library of Congress.

British Library Cataloguing in Publication Data
A CIP catalogue record for this book is available from the British Library.

ISBN 978 1 84905 520 8
eISBN 978 0 85700 940 1

Printed and bound in Great Britain

This book is dedicated to my dear family and friends who were a great support to me whilst co-writing this book. A special dedication to my father, Neville, who was a true inspiration.

Matthew Graham

Much appreciation and thanks to all those that have influenced my thinking, shared their knowledge and experience and ensured my passion for advocacy, the Mental Capacity Act and all its intricacies grows each day. Thank you to my parents for supporting me in all I do and of course to my husband Mark, for everything.

Jakki Cowley

Contents

Chapter 5   Advance Care Planning

Chapter 6   Best Interests

Chapter 7   Liberty and Choice

Foreword

The Mental Capacity Act 2005 (MCA 2005) is a visionary piece of legislation, which, as the House of Lords Select Committee convened to consider its implementation noted, 'signified a step change in the legal rights afforded to those who may lack capacity, with the potential to transform the lives of many' (House of Lords Select Committee House of Lords Select Committee on the MCA 2005 Post-Legislative Scrutiny Report, March 2014). However, as the same Committee noted:

> Its implementation has not met the expectations that it rightly raised. The Act has suffered from a lack of awareness and a lack of understanding. For many who are expected to comply with the Act it appears to be an optional add-on, far from being central to their working lives. The evidence presented to us concerns the health and social care sectors principally. In those sectors the prevailing cultures of paternalism (in health) and risk-aversion (in social care) have prevented the Act from becoming widely known or embedded. The empowering ethos has not been delivered. The rights conferred by the Act have not been widely realised. The duties imposed by the Act are not widely followed.

The message of the Select Committee is therefore clear: all those who are concerned – in whatever context – with seeking to enable those whose capacity may be in doubt to take their own decisions or, where they truly cannot, to take decisions in their best interests need all the help that they can get in internalising the principles of the Act and applying them in practice.

Jakki Cowley and Matthew Graham have set themselves an ambitious task: to attempt to demystify the MCA 2005 and to make key aspects workable in practice. Bringing their great collective expertise in the application of the MCA 2005 to bear, they have succeeded triumphantly. With clarity, wisdom and, above all, practical insight they have written a book which does far more than repeat the law (or the Codes of Practice accompanying the Act) in different words, but actually seeks to explain what the law means and what proper application looks like in practice.

Bolstered by a plethora of case studies, checklists and other practical tools, the book provides vital – and much needed – guidance for anyone concerned with seeking to apply the Act in a whole host of situations. It should be required reading and I hope that it will find its way onto the bookshelves of anyone who really cares about this extraordinarily important but so-often misunderstood piece of legislation.

Alex Ruck Keene
Barrister, Thirty Nine Essex Street
Honorary Research Lecturer at the University of Manchester
7 November 2014

Acknowledgments

The authors wish to thank Debbie Divine, Mr and Mrs E, Annie Ho, Lynn Hodges, Louise Jessup, Mary Macdonald, Alex Ruck Keene and Andy Wall for their insights into the Mental Capacity Act, which have helped to construct this book. The authors are also grateful for permission to reproduce documentation created by the Kent and Medway MCA Local Implementation Network. A special thanks to Stephen Jones and all at Jessica Kingsley Publishers for the opportunity to write this book and for help and encouragement along the way.

Introduction

The Mental Capacity Act 2005 (MCA) came onto the statute books for England and Wales in 2007 and is undoubtedly one of the most significant pieces of law that directly applies to adults, carers, family members, health and social care professionals and the legal profession in equal measure by discussing people's rights, choices, best interests and how care ought to be considered, decided upon and delivered in certain circumstances.

The MCA, however, is first and foremost about people who are aged 16 and above who lack the mental capacity to make specific decisions for themselves at specific times. The Act offers a framework for lawful, ethical and value-laden practice that encompasses person-centred care, empowerment, values diversity, respects choices and enables people to make their own decisions through maximizing capacity. There are two exceptions, however, as to when the MCA applies to people under the age of 16. These are in relation to the Court of Protection making decisions about a child's property or finances (or appoint a deputy to do so) if the child lacks capacity to make such decisions. The second is that section 44 of the MCA (offences of ill-treatment or wilful neglect of a person who lacks capacity) can also apply to individuals under the age of 16.

The MCA is primarily about people's rights to make decisions and choices and their rights to have decisions and choices made for them in their best interests if they lack the mental capacity to be able to make these decisions for themselves. The issues and dilemmas primarily arise in managing the tensions that come from balancing these two key concepts when they arise in practice. Carers in residential care homes and judges in the Court of Protection will often find themselves making decisions in a person's best interests, but what is often forgotten is that the process for both parties is the same – they are both applying the MCA by considering the MCA's principles and by reflecting on the Act itself and the Code of Practice.

The MCA consists of 69 sections over three parts and contains schedules and regulations, covering a whole plethora of topics, some of which are more exclusive to certain situations and practitioners than others – one of the schedules (A1) being the Deprivation of Liberty Safeguards. When considering law, health and social care, practitioners can often lack confidence and feel concern in relation to what they should know and how they should implement it. Quite often there is an additional concern in relation to how practitioners can find out what it is they need to know. Good practice is not about being told what to do and then going ahead and doing it. People and their circumstances are not only more complex than following such a superficial process, but actually deserve deeper and wider reflection in relation to their capacity, rights, choices and decision-making.

There is no expectation for practitioners to know every section of the MCA and to be able to quote it verbatim; this would not only be impossible, but would also be unnecessary as not all sections of the Act apply to all situations. This is not to suggest that practitioners should 'cherry pick' what they need to know and apply it with undue consideration and regards to people's welfare, but it does mean that the 'spirit of the MCA' is what all should be aiming to achieve in order to demonstrate in their practice an understanding and due regard of people, their care, uniqueness and self-determination.

The spirit of the MCA is what this book is all about and the seven chapters reflect the most common points that arise in day-to-day care in care homes, hospitals, people's own homes and a whole range of other care provisions up and down the nation. Not only is this book essential reading for care home staff and managers, nurses, doctors and managers in hospitals, but also for social workers, care managers, advocates, family members and carers and, of course, people who use services.

When we consider the term 'service users' or 'people who use services' we are not referring to an exclusive group of people who might use specialist services; the mentioning of service users is not to 'other' people nor distance them from the wider readership of this book. In relation to this book the term 'service user' means everybody, because we *all* use health and social care services (and beyond) where capacity is considered on a daily basis. We are all likely to visit a GP or dentist, optician or need to consent to care or treatment in hospital, even for the most minor of circumstances. Capacity is a topic that affects all of us at any given time, and those to whom we entrust our care will be mindful of our capacity as much as we are of those for whom we care.

Mental capacity does not mean a 'mental health difficulty' or having a 'learning disability' or receiving care as an 'older person'. These are unhelpful stereotypes that a misunderstanding of the MCA has created over the eight years since its inception. Mental capacity is the ability to make a decision and as we read throughout this book it is in relation to any impairment and/or disturbance in the functioning of the mind or brain. This may be due to one of the above aforementioned labels, but not necessarily. Just as any of us may need to consent to treatment and have our capacity assessed, we are also likely to experience a lack of capacity at any point due to an impairment or disturbance in the functioning of the mind or brain. It is highly unlikely that anyone reading this book has never lost capacity as the MCA suggests. You may have had one too many alcoholic drinks, sustained a head injury following a cycling accident, had a fever resulting in a confused state or have been unconscious. These are all examples of where you may have lacked mental capacity to make a decision due to an impairment and/or disturbance in the functioning of the mind or brain. Therefore, this book applies to everyone who is reading it right now.

Having said that, there is a point to this book that is a little clearer than that and finely honed towards a specific purpose. That purpose was discovered over a period of time in the work that we have undertaken as teaching and training specialists in the Mental Capacity Act. Much of the work that we have undertaken has involved providing teaching and training to all kinds of staff in health and social care over a number of years and providing specialist consultancy work on the MCA to all types of agencies from small care homes and large hospital Trusts through to social services teams and people who use services through to the Department of Health.

What has consistently come across in the contacts we have made over the years is that many practitioners want the MCA and

Code of Practice demystified. Neither of us are lawyers, nor do we offer legal advice, but between us we have many years of practice and teaching in health and social care and have more stories than can be recalled in relation to good and bad practice. One consistent message that has come from the work we do is to have accessible information as to what the MCA 'looks like' in practice and to offer something which the readership can easily digest and apply in practice in order to enhance the experiences of people who require support with making decisions or who require decisions to be made for them in their best interests. Equally, this book is also about enhancing the experiences of practitioners by enabling them to grasp the concept of the MCA and for it to be a helpful, workable tool that serves to instill confidence and reassurance in the important work that they do.

This book is not a law book – it is a book about what the law looks like in practice and the chapters aim to cover what most practitioners will want to consider in practice. This book does not aim to replace the Act itself, nor the Codes of Practice for the MCA and Deprivation of Liberty Safeguards (DoLS) in relation to offering guidance. The primary source of guidance should always be these sources and any specific legal advice should be sought from an appropriate legal source who is qualified to offer that advice.

This book does, however, offer a practical guide that hopes to demystify the MCA and make key aspects workable in practice. We offer case scenarios for practitioners to reflect upon as well as grids, forms and practical tools that can be used in practice to aid tasks and work undertaken. This book also offers reassurance to people as to what their rights are and how they should expect to receive certain care and treatment. It is hoped that this book will act to facilitate individuals to gain confidence in practice and know how to challenge poor practice. But this book is not about poor practice, nor is it about criticizing poor practice. It's primarily about what good practice should look like, and that service providers should celebrate that when they know they are doing what's required lawfully, ethically and whilst keeping the person who lacks capacity at the centre of their decision-making. This book is not a textbook that aims to reflect upon the views of other authors (hence the few references) but is a guide that primarily offers the authors' thoughts and advice on what should be considered, when it should be considered and how it should be considered.

Within the MCA the letter 'P' is used to refer to the person who lacks capacity or is being supported to make a decision. Therefore, this book will follow suit and will occasionally use this abbreviation to refer to the key person to whom this book primarily applies.

Capacity will always remain a contentious issue in practice and it is suggested that the primary focus of the MCA is not about how to make decisions for people who lack capacity, but is about developing cultures of care that serve to maximize people's capacity, support their decision-making and advocate for them so that their voice is heard, opinions upheld and rights enhanced. Of course, there will be times when we do need to make decisions for people in their best interests and this book offers guidance on that so that practitioners can act with confidence in relation to the law, but essentially, so that vulnerable adults remain the focus and inspiration of the good practice that we aim to deliver on a daily basis.

We are grateful to all those we have met over the years – people who use services, family members, carers and practitioners who have truly inspired us in all we do. This book and its contents is shaped by their stories, their experiences and dilemmas, but also their celebrations, knowledge, skills and values. This book is about them and our continual drive to raise the profile of the MCA in practice so that it inspires care of exceptional quality.

Matt Graham and Jakki Cowley
October 2014

Chapter 1

A New Culture of Care

There is a reason why you are reading this book and that reason is, we hope, because you want to be reading it rather than because you have to and that you have an interest in mental capacity and people's choices, autonomy and self-determination.

When legislation and policy is considered, we can often be propelled into thinking that certain 'rules and regulations' need to be applied in practice because of our obligation to do just that and, to a degree, this is correct, but the spirit of the Mental Capacity Act 2005 is to provide a framework that governs, supports and upholds the principles of choice and self-determination in people's decision-making and enables practitioners, family members and carers to make decisions for people who lack capacity in their best interests. The MCA is about human rights, dignity and enablement – concepts that ought to transcend legislation and be central within the good practice of the caring professions.

The Mental Capacity Act 2005 (MCA) came into force in 2007 and applies to anyone in England and Wales who is aged 16 and above, although it is worth noting that it also applies to people aged under 16 in two contexts, as stated earlier. The MCA provides a framework to empower and protect people who may lack capacity to make some decisions for themselves and makes clear who can make decisions for others and in which situations, and how they should go about this. Anyone who works with or cares for an adult who lacks capacity must comply with the MCA when making decisions or acting for that person (Ministry of Justice 2014). The MCA also seeks to ensure that people's capacity is maximized and they are supported to make decisions.

The MCA is undoubtedly the only piece of legislation in England and Wales that in the very first section, right at the beginning, sets out what the entire Act is about. It offers us the 'The Principles', sometimes referred to as The Five Principles or Five Key Principles. These are:

1. A person must be assumed to have capacity unless it is established he lacks capacity.

2. A person is not to be treated as unable to make a decision unless all practicable steps to help him do so have been taken without success.

3. A person is not to be treated as unable to make a decision merely because he makes an unwise decision.

4. An act done, or decision made, under this Act for or on behalf of a person who lacks capacity must be done, or made, in his best interests.

5. Before the act is done, or the decision is made, regard must be had to whether the purpose for which it is needed can be as effectively achieved in a way that is less restrictive of the person's rights and freedom of action.

These five principles will be discussed throughout the book as they fully encompass the spirit of the MCA.

In 2012 NHS England published *Compassion in Practice*, a three-year vision and strategy for nursing, midwifery and care staff drawn up by Jane Cummings, the Chief Nursing Officer for England (CNO) at the NHS Commissioning Board, and Viv Bennett, Director of Nursing at the Department of Health. Through consultation with staff, patients and carers this three-year vision drew up what is known as the *6 Cs*:

- Care
- Compassion
- Competence
- Communication
- Courage
- Commitment.

(www.england.nhs.uk 2012)

The tension for practitioners and carers when considering cultures of care is that everyone has an opinion on what 'good care' should look like. The question is, are there any absolute definitions of what 'good care' entails? If the care individuals receive ought to be based upon people's individuality, choices and preferences – whilst practitioners and carers uphold the spirit of P's self-determination – then we start to develop ideas of the underpinning values that constitute good care. Our argument then swiftly becomes one that is value and ethically driven rather than concrete in terms of establishing what a good culture of care actually 'is'. This is where the term 'culture' comes into its own inasmuch as helping us to define concepts of care and how those entrusted to our care should be treated. We are outraged, and quite rightly so, when people receive anything less than good care and there are clear standards of practice expected within hospitals, care homes and people's own homes. But when standards slip, mistakes are made and individuals are neglected where do we assign the locus of blame? With the individual carer? The organization? The state? Or do we actually enter into the discourse in relation to cultures of care? There are times when clear failings can be located in specific places because the evidence of inquiry establishes that and the following discussions and reactions may well serve to critique certain practices and might even bring about positive change, but what is important is that society is able to enter into the debate around why certain practices are good in some places and not so good elsewhere. When we consider the term 'culture of care' we ought to remain mindful of what it suggests, how it is interpreted and what the MCA offers in relation to considering this concept.

This chapter will aim to guide the reader through the construction of the term and make connections with good practice.

When we consider culture we may consider and reflect upon 'the way things are' within any area of knowledge and what thinking and practices underpin that knowledge (Trevithick 2012). For example, practitioners' views around how care is delivered may be based upon western ideology, upbringing, acquired values, religion, and any other factor which may influence an individual's understanding of a person's needs and how to respond to those needs. However, when the term 'culture of care' is considered it is suggested that our considerations should broaden beyond our own perspectives of how we view certain phenomena. We have to balance this with the organization's perspectives and culture, but most importantly, that of the person. It is only when we consider these perspectives and make attempts to balance them do we start to experience tension. It is this very tension that can be a key determinant in the process of applying reflective, person-centred practice or undesirable and even abusive practice. Tension in any given setting causes us to react and can propel us into specific modes of intervening.

Organizational culture

In February 2010, Sir Robert Francis QC reviewed the failings of the Mid Staffordshire NHS Foundation Trust between the periods of 2005–2009. The Francis report highlights 'a systematic failure of the provisions of good care.' Throughout his report Robert Francis noted failings in care ranging from patients being left soiled in their own excrement in their hospital beds, through to senior hospital managers not paying attention to staff concerns as a result of being too heavily focused on targets. Ultimately the report concludes that within the hospital Trust there was 'an insidious negative culture involving a tolerance of poor standards and a disengagement from managerial and leadership responsibilities.' There is no doubt that this was a damning report which shook the NHS to its core and filled patients and carers with concerns about levels of 'basic' care in hospitals and whether care that just did not meet even adequate standards was in fact the default position.

Certainly, the Francis Report is a not the result of an inquiry that should be considered alone, but regarded within the wider scope of care and organizations, such as care homes, for example. This does not, of course, mean to say that we should think all organizations will cause vulnerable people harm and that, by virtue of being a public or private body providing care in the UK, that harm will automatically follow. This is not what is being suggested here at all, in fact on the contrary, but what is being suggested is that organizations by very nature of being organizations can quickly develop pervasive and undesirable traits which can become accepted quickly as 'the norm' through the process of certain practices being drip fed into practitioners' thinking as acceptable when they are clearly not. But the question that this generates is, if it is clear to us that certain levels of care are just not acceptable, then why is not always clear to those involved in delivering the care?

Winterbourne View

Six care workers at the Winterbourne View care home were given prison terms on Friday for 'cruel, callous and degrading' abuse of disabled patients.

The judge at Bristol crown court also condemned five other staff members at the private home in Hambrook, South Gloucestershire, who received suspended sentences. Judge Neil Ford told the defendants their behaviour triggered 'widespread feelings of revulsion'.

The 11 defendants – nine support workers and two nurses – admitted 38 charges of either neglect or ill-treatment of five people with severe learning difficulties after being secretly recorded by a reporter for the BBC's Panorama programme.

They were filmed slapping extremely vulnerable residents, soaking them in water, trapping them under chairs, taunting and swearing at them, pulling their hair and poking their eyes. Whistleblower Terry Bryan, a former nurse at the home, contacted the BBC after his warnings were ignored by Castlebeck Ltd, which owned the hospital, and care watchdogs.

(The Guardian, 26 October 2012)

The MCA offers something of great importance

When reflecting upon the culture of care and standards of care within care organizations it would be unhelpful to construct an argument on the over-simplistic principles of 'good care' and 'bad care' as very few hospitals and care homes would ever admit to offering poor care. But there is an argument to be made in relation to how poor care can easily become part of P's day-to-day life because it has infiltrated the culture of the organizations, not necessarily because anyone has made a conscious decision to start abusing someone or to ill-treat them but because what the MCA now offers people, whether they have capacity or not to make a particular decision, is a foundation on which to build certain principles that will, if consciously practised, enter the value base of a practitioner's judgement and therefore start to shape the care offered to the benefit of the person, family/carers and practitioners alike.

Where were we before the MCA?

The question of 'where were we before the MCA?' is an important question to ask when reflecting upon where organizations ought to be and hopefully want to be in relation to good practice and applying the spirit of the Act. In order to know where we want to be it is often helpful to consider where we have come from.

Autonomy

Prior to the MCA people's autonomy was not always respected and people who appeared to have a learning disability or who had a diagnosis of dementia, for example, may well have been written-off by professionals as incapable of making decisions and therefore were offered very few opportunities to express their wishes and preferences and make choices. Therefore within the spirit of the MCA it is important to ensure that all individuals are able to express their autonomy in relation to decision-making and be able to make judgments around decisions that have an impact on their lives. Autonomy is a key factor for people in living their lives free from control at worst, and paternalistic attitudes at best. Even though there might be a sense to 'do the right thing' for people in our care it is an absolute imperative that P is supported to demonstrate individual judgement and have that liberty, through the process of the MCA, to step away from controlling care. Lack of involvement in decision-making increases the dependency of people and reduces their autonomy (Ferns 2012 in Tew (ed.) 2012).

What is concerning, however, is that by over-riding people's autonomy in relation to decision-making as care providers, we end up reinforcing stigma by creating stereotypes of people who receive care as being passive recipients of care and having no say over what they do and when they do it.

Authority

We would be forgiven for thinking that the current climate in relation to risk, risk assessment and associated risk aversion might result in practitioners concluding that there is great concern in supporting people who use services, particularly in care homes, to make autonomous decisions, albeit that there may well be great practice demonstrated in relation to maximizing capacity and supporting decision-making.

Case study

Mandip is 28 years old and lives in a small residential care home with three other people. He has a learning disability and gets on fairly well with the staff who work in the home, although staff shortages have resulted in agency staff being called upon fairly frequently, which causes Mandip some upset and concern as he doesn't know them and is quite anxious around strangers.

Mandip really enjoys going over the road to the shop to buy sweets and saying hello to the staff who work there and who know him well. He always goes over with staff from the care home because of his difficulties crossing the road and his lack of understanding in relation to road safety.

On this occasion when Mandip wishes to go out, there is only one agency member of staff available who cannot leave the other service users in order to take him.

Mandip decides that he will go out anyway, but is prevented from doing so by the agency staff member who says that he can go out as soon as another member of staff comes in, in about an hour. The staff member guides Mandip back into the house and shuts the door behind him. Mandip is unhappy about this and says he will tell his mum that he was stopped from going out.

There is nothing particularly unusual about this scenario, in that this is a fairly common occurrence in many care homes, but in light of this common occurrence there is a question that staff often fail to ask themselves, but must do so in order to ensure that they remain mindful of not only the MCA but also P's rights, self-determination and autonomy. When a member of staff makes a decision such as this they should not necessarily be asking themselves whether the decision they are making is the 'right' or 'wrong' decision, but they ought to ask themselves...

'On what authority am I making this decision?'

The paternalistic culture of care requires challenging at all levels, but must first be reflected upon by the individual care provider. We simply cannot care for people in ways that control, undermine and exert authority over others, least not when that authority actually doesn't exist. Of course, people need to feel safe and receive care that enables and promotes their safety and wellbeing, but in itself the concept of safeguarding can engender an ethos within the practice of care providers that this involves making decisions for and over people.

Considering a biopsychosocial approach can actually help in such matters by offering an holisitic view on people's care, wellbeing and safety. In the above example of Mandip the decision made may well have been a natural decision for a member of staff to make in such a circumstance, so from a *biological* perspective Mandip's physical health may well be secured by preventing him from going out at that time due to not being able to provide him with the support to cross the road. Therefore, he remains in the home in safety. Nevertheless, *psychologically* this may well have a detrimentally significant impact upon him as he may feel low about this and disheartened by being prevented from doing what he wants to do. In turn, Mandip's *social* identity might experience stigma due to the process of labeling, stereotyping and separating (Thornicroft 2007) which has naturally occurred through the process of wanting to *safeguard* him. Unconsciously, the staff member may well have labeled Mandip as being unsafe if he were to leave the home unaccompanied. Such continual practices can lead to care organizations stereotyping groups of people with unhealthy and unhelpful characteristics, such as, 'People who have a learning disability need keeping an eye on,' this can then lead to a process of 'othering' people as society separates them as 'not being one of us'. This is a powerful and oppressive process but one that has increasingly become the 'norm' in our culture of care, particularly demonstrated in the care of adults who have a learning disability or dementia type illness.

The need to safeguard people and protect them is a requirement for practice, but must be viewed much deeper and wider than merely preventing people from doing something that it is considered will cause them harm. Therefore this requirement must be balanced against the necessity to uphold people's rights, autonomy and self-determination.

People who cannot express their current wishes and feelings in words may express themselves through their behaviour. Expressions of pleasure or distress and emotional responses will also be relevant when working out what is in their best interests. It is also important to be able to ensure that other people have not influenced a person's view...
Code of Practice, Chapter 5.40

Reflecting on the above chapter of the Code of Practice will support practitioners to locate meaning for individuals within their practice by encouraging staff to consider what P is communicating beyond the limitations of speech, through behaviour and emotions.

We have briefly considered the concept of authority to act in this chapter, and it is hoped that this provides some confidence to carers and professionals to think beyond the realms of 'the right thing to do' within practice, but we will now take a look at a particular issue that over the years has ever increasingly become a part of the culture of care, particularly within inpatient hospital settings. This is the issue of *implied consent*.

Why has the term implied consent been used here rather than 'consent'? There is a very clear reason for this and that is because this discussion needs to focus on specific practice and what the spirit of the MCA has to say about this. Practice issues in relation to implied consent seem to present more challenges than simply the consideration of consent, *per se*.

Implied consent...really?

The NHS, as the largest health employer in the nation, is very clear in relation to what it means by consent.

Consent to treatment is the principle that a person must give their permission before they receive any type of medical treatment or examination. This must be done on the basis of a preliminary explanation by a clinician.

Consent is required from a patient regardless of the intervention – from a physical examination to organ donation.

The principle of consent is an important part of medical ethics and the international human rights law.

It can be given:

1. Verbally – for example, by saying they are happy to have an X-ray.

2. In writing – for example, by signing a consent form for surgery.

Patients may passively allow treatment to take place – for example, by holding out an arm to show they are happy to have a blood test. However, since the capacity to consent has not been tested, and the benefits and risks have not been explained, this is not the same as consent.

NHS (2014)

Best interests principles are enshrined within the MCA in its entirety (see Chapter 6), so this tells us that we must consider the concept of best interests beyond the realms of section 4 of the Act and best interests meetings. Good practice has always considered what is in P's best interests and those who seek to not act in P's best interests should not be working with vulnerable people.

Critical analysis and reflection will help practitioners to consider how best care is delivered and to become increasingly confident and competent in delivering care and seeking consent. However, seeking consent is not a straightforward process such as identifying whether P says 'yes' or 'no' in relation to care and treatment offered, and consent is most certainly not given by P signing a piece of paper to agree to a particular course of action. As with all decisions in relation to care, the first principle of the MCA must be remembered, that P must be assumed to have mental capacity unless it is established that they lack capacity. So, if an individual consents to treatment based on having all the information and options offered to them so as to be able to make a decision, and there is no evidence to suggest they lack capacity, then the practitioner can proceed and deliver the treatment. They must be very clear in their own mind that it is P who has made the best interests decision and it is merely the practitioner who is delivering that on P's authority.

However, it becomes less clear to the practitioner if P is deemed to lack capacity but does not appear to object to the care or treatment. It is suggested that it is only perceived to be less clear, because the cloud of uncertainty blurs the sight of confident practice; the reality is that this issue *is* perfectly clear because the MCA is perfectly clear about it. First, let us for a moment consider Freda.

Case study
Freda is 82 years old and is in hospital following a fall at home. She has a diagnosis of dementia and numerous physical health ailments. Due to Freda's difficulties she speaks very little, and when she does it can be difficult to understand her, which leads to Freda becoming distressed and staff confused. However, Freda is very compliant with the care she is receiving and clearly shows feelings of pleasure or distress through her behaviour and facial expressions.

The nurses need to take blood from Freda as part of routine tests, but when approached by one of the nurses Freda puts her arm out and the blood is taken quickly and successfully. Freda does not appeared bothered by this and all is well.

A nursing student who is on placement asked the nurse whether Freda consented to the procedure. The nurse replied by saying that the injection was given through implied consent.

Implied consent is not a concept that is supported within this book, purely because no practitioner has any right to determine what is believed in terms of what people say. P either consents or does not. Informed consent is also a term this book does not support, purely because unless someone has all the information available to them to make a decision then they are not able to consent. Therefore consent is actually a process, not an outcome – without necessary information given to P and consent not being given by P, then the practitioner may well be proceeding with P's care unethically and, most certainly, unprofessionally.

When considering consent, practitioners must remain mindful of the first principle of the five statutory principles – the presumption of capacity. If there is nothing to suggest that P lacks the capacity to consent, then the presumption of capacity stands and practitioners must understand that it is P who has decided what is in their best interests and therefore can consent to or not agree to certain care or treatment. If there is evidence to suggest that P lacks the capacity to make that decision based upon an assessment of capacity (which must be recorded) then usual processes are followed by the person who is delivering the care and treatment acting as the decision-maker and proceeding to act in P's best interests (see Chapter 6).

What we need to try and avoid, however, in practice is this idea that we can guess whether P is consenting or not. We also cannot assume that just because someone is not objecting to something then they are necessarily consenting. But in this case of Freda (above) there is no evidence to suggest she lacks the capacity to make that decision, so the presumption of capacity stands and it is recorded that Freda consented because she offered her arm. Nothing in her expressions or behaviour suggested she was distressed or under duress and no form of coercion or restraint was used. Using the term 'implied consent' leaves the practitioner open to a whole range of challenges and disputes, but most importantly, leaves P vulnerable to the ongoing and perhaps ever-increasing culture of care that we can presume P's consent and proceed with all decisions on that basis. It is for these reasons that we have the MCA on our statute books and why it actually attempts to instill confidence in practitioners, if they actually allow this to happen.

The power dynamic

The paradox of care is that concepts of empowerment are debatable and should actually be critically considered. The MCA is a piece of legislation that places P at the centre of all it enshrines. We do not place P there because they are already there. Let us not be so arrogant as to think it is our decision to permit someone to make a decision – that level of care would actually espouse totalitarianism within the culture of care homes and hospitals and send the message that professionals are all powerful and that people who use services are merely the recipients of what that care involves. The increasing and most welcome rise of the experts by experience movement into decision-making bodies, university teaching teams and policy writing is resulting in the power dynamic shifting towards equal decision-making and people who use services having a place at the table.

A practice interaction

Empowering, she wrote!

'I empowered David to consider the options...'

'My work with the service user was empowering...'

'Rita was empowered to apply for a part-time job.'

You're the powerful one, he wrote!

'Please consider your use of language and how you are portraying yourself as the dominant powerful force by choosing who you give the gift of empowerment to...if that actually exists!'

The above example is fictional, but certainly gives an insight into how a practitioner or a student might have dialogue with a more experienced practitioner or tutor in relation to an understanding of 'empowerment'.

Empowerment, as a concept, is a hot topic. It's a buzzword and is used freely within practice to regularly lubricate the wheels of emancipatory interventions by practitioners reassuring themselves of their best intentions to empower people, but does this practice actually exist? Can it exist? Surely, only those who use services can actually determine the experiences and levels of empowerment that are felt and experienced. Thus, it is suggested that empowerment is a subjective concept that only has a life as it is experienced by the individual.

The power of empowerment lies with the person to therefore empower themselves through the support and provision of the practitioner. This tells us something very important indeed – it tells us that practitioners do not empower people at all. Practitioners can only support the person and work with them to be at the place where they can empower themselves. Critics of this might argue that, surely, enabling someone to a place is empowering them, but we must not get lost in the murky mire of semantics and, in fact, enter freely into the discourse that if it is within a practitioner's choosing to empower someone, then this is an awfully powerful position to be in and one that in doing so actually makes P less powerful.

Quite often the power dynamic is seen within care homes by how staff view where they work. Is your organization someone's home that you work in, or is it your place of employment that someone lives in? This might seem like a silly question, but it is one that shines a light on attitudes and values and is helpful to ask in order to explore the answers together.

Person-centred practice

Quite often practitioners are asking themselves this question, a question which managers of services want an answer to...

'How can I show compliance with the MCA?'

When the MCA first entered the statute books in October of 2007, the question that was asked by practitioners and the inspectorate alike was in relation to awareness of the MCA. Certainly, trainers and consultants who specialized in the MCA delivered 'awareness' training. As time moved on 'awareness' became less of an issue and 'compliance' was the key to understanding how the MCA is applied in practice. Having an awareness of legislation and policy is all to the good but it will only be 'seen' in practice if compliance is present.

Confidence and competence in relation to the MCA should not be confused, inasmuch as suggesting that practitioners do not need to know every section of the Act and every chapter of the Code of Practice and be able to quote this verbatim. This is quite simply not a requirement, so having competence of the law is not so much a necessity as having confidence in your knowledge of the *spirit of the Act*. But what precisely does this mean? What does the new culture of care in relation to the MCA tell us? This books suggests that the spirit of the MCA is defined as such…

People and their right to make decisions is at the centre of the MCA. All must be done to promote and enhance people's choice, autonomy and self-determination. Equally, decision-makers must demonstrate confidence and clarity in how decisions in people's best interests are reached for those who do not have the capacity to make a decision for themselves at any given time.

The above suggestion of the spirit of the MCA tells us that the MCA is, rather simplistically, about two things and two things only:

1. People's rights to make decisions.
2. People's rights to have decisions made for them if they lack the capacity to make the decision themselves.

Confidence, competence and compliance with the MCA can be demonstrated if practitioners know the differences between the two and can remain mindful of the tensions that exist when trying to work out that difference. Compliance with the MCA is not simply about doing things 'to' people, or 'for' them or even 'with' them but rather it is about ensuring that we fully uphold the presumption of capacity, seek all opportunities to maximize capacity and support decision-making and be confident to intervene and make decisions for that person if it is felt necessary, at that time, because P lacks the capacity to make a decision.

The MCA is a piece of safeguarding legislation, but it is also a piece of legislation that if considered as it should, is utterly emancipatory. Emancipation in its literal sense means to 'free' someone – to emancipate them, to provide liberty! The MCA offers people freedom in decision-making, the freedom to be able to say to others, 'These are my wishes and values and this is the decision that I want to make.' Of course, the skill in understanding law and applying it also suggests that when people are unable to make those decisions through an impairment or disturbance in the functioning of their mind or brain, that others continue to think of how making best interests decisions can also be an emancipatory act by enabling the person to receive the care/treatment/decision that needs to be made for them, and which they wouldn't be able to receive in any other way.

Responsibilities at all levels

This chapter makes references to practitioners and those providing care at the ground level. Standards of practice are quite clear that those delivering care remain responsible and accountable for the delivery of their own care, therefore individual responsibility is key in understanding requirements, standards and the knowledge, skills and values of good practice. Nevertheless, numerous serious case reviews, legal judgments and inquiries over the years have made reference to corporate responsibilities and this, so called, culture of care. Section 44 of the MCA, which makes it a criminal offence to ill-treat or willfully neglect a person who lacks capacity to make relevant decisions if you have the care of that person is aimed at:

> Capturing those individuals who are in a position of trust, care or power over people who are then ill-treated or neglected. That could be a donee of a lasting power of attorney, a deputy appointed by the court or a person who has the care of a person who lacks capacity, such as a member of staff in a hospital or care home or family member. (Parliamentary-Under Secretary of State, St. Comm. A, col.383, in Jones 2012)

The statement above refers to individuals, but what happened at Winterbourne View and what the Francis Report into Mid Staffordshire NHS Trust tells us is that there were failings at all levels and that, over a period of time, neglectful practice became the 'norm' as impressionable staff were influenced by more powerful staff and managers failed to hear the concerns from those who were clearly expressing them.

'What can't be cured must be endured' is the very worst and most dangerous maxim for a nurse which ever was made. Patience and resignation are but other words for carelessness and indifference – contemptible if in regard to herself; culpable if in regard to her sick.
Florence Nightingale, Notes on Nursing (1860), pp.92–93 (Cited in Francis 2013)

These very words written by Florence Nightingale 155 years ago are as meaningful today as they were then, if not even more so. This idea that what can't be cured must be endured is indeed a maxim of dangerousness, particularly when it comes to enduring, or putting up with poor standards of care. Up and down the nation there are care homes and hospitals and care people receive at home which are of an exceptionally high standard, but what determines what is 'high' or 'good' or 'adequate' or 'poor'? It's the default position. If we come to expect average or poor then anything other than this will be seen as, quite often, excellent! What is required, perhaps, is that we lose the overuse of adjectives to describe care (Care Quality Commission [CQC], please note!) and start to construct sentences that are meaningful to those who use services and make sense to carers and relatives. Receiving 'excellent' care might be quite meaningless and even lead to this resignation of indifference that Florence Nightingale referred to, because can it get any better? What comes above excellent? Very excellent? Care must always improve by seeking greater levels and examples of person-centred care, valuing diversity and self-determination, staff advocating for people's wishes and preferences (as the person has identified them) and remaining constantly mindful of people's best interests and duty to consult with others in order to build knowledge and greater understanding around the person's needs.

Cultures of care, failings in delivering care of sufficient standard and acts of ill-treatment and willful neglect can and do enter into *acts of omission* as well as care that goes out with the purpose of harming an individual (as clearly seen in Winterbourne View). The Social Care Institute for Excellence (SCIE) (2014) defines an act of omission as:

The failure of any person, who has responsibility for the charge, care or custody of an adult at risk, to provide the amount and type of care that a reasonable person would be expected to provide. Neglect can be intentional or unintentional.

A police officer who was also the investigating officer in an adult safeguarding case once said, 'Ill-treatment is relatively easy to define, as is neglect, but willful neglect? That's quite tough. How do you prove willful? The alleged perpetrator won't usually admit to it.' This generated an interesting discussion around intention v acts of omission and the result was that not being mindful of the MCA and not given the care and treatment that someone who lacks capacity can be willful neglect. Ignorance of the law acts as no defence and a failure to comply with the MCA may well establish a *breach* of a duty of care owed by a carer. The intention here is not to scare practitioners, but to prompt them that the MCA's sole purpose is to offer a safeguard mechanism and support practitioners in delivering that.

Case study

A 999 call was made to a care home for older adults due to Mrs Harris falling over in her bedroom. She hit her head very badly on the bedside table and was clearly concussed. She had a deep wound in her head and staff had managed to stem the blood loss with towels. Mrs Harris was highly confused and the bang to her head had clearly had an impact upon her judgement, in addition to causing physical damage.

When the ambulance arrived Mrs Harris clearly needed to go to A&E to receive assessment, care and treatment, but she refused to go, stating she wanted to remain at home as she was fine. All the evidence suggested that Mrs Harris lacked the mental capacity to make the decision (see Chapter 3) at that time and that the decision (which was to take her to hospital) could not be delayed. Nevertheless, due to her forthright and articulate expression of not wishing to go, ambulance staff left her at the home once the blood loss had ceased, informing care home staff that they couldn't make someone go to hospital against their will. The ambulance crew left, without Mrs Harris.

It is worth remembering that there is this myth in practice that appears to be part of the culture of care that practitioners cannot act if someone refuses. This, of course, does not mean to say that the MCA states we can override people's rights and make decisions because we feel we ought to – on the contrary, in fact. But it does highlight that the MCA has much to say about what can be done in a situation like this so as to ensure that Mrs Harris would not be neglected and that she would receive the care that she appears to need. Here are some points in relation to the above case which must be considered and aligned with the understanding of cultures of care and competent and confident practice:

- Mrs Harris is assumed to have capacity unless there is evidence to the contrary. All attempts will be made to maximize her capacity (see Chapter 2).

- Mrs Harris has an impairment or disturbance in the functioning of her mind or brain and there are clear triggers to assess her capacity. Her capacity is assessed (see Chapter 3).

- Mrs Harris' carers in the care home know her well and advocate her needs to the ambulance crew and consult with family members (see Chapter 4).

- Mrs Harris' wishes and preferences are documented in her care plan within the home and this is discussed by care home staff and the ambulance crew. She has not written any advance decision to refuse treatment (see Chapter 5).

- Despite Mrs Harris refusing treatment has any consideration been given to what is in Mrs Harris' best interests? Is Mrs Harris able to determine what is in her own best interests? (see Chapter 6).

- Mrs Harris' situation is potentially problematic for her with her head injury. There is some tension between her refusal to go to hospital and the imperative to uphold her rights. But doesn't she also have the right to receive care and treatment? The MCA permits the use of reasonable and proportionate force in exceptional circumstances if it is in someone's best interests if they lack capacity and the criteria are met. But the criteria must be met and this action must be given much consideration (see Chapter 7).

The new culture of care that the MCA has created actually stems from pre-existing good practice, duties of care and unwritten rules as to what good care should 'look like'. Although major inquiries into failings in care are rare, it is probably the case that the MCA not being considered in practice as a matter of course is rare. But what Mrs Harris' circumstances (above) tell us is that the MCA applies to many situations if we just take the time to consider it and remain mindful of it. Managers providing good supervision to staff so as to regularly reflect with staff on good practice should be supporting staff to consider:

1. **Ethically driven practice:** This goes beyond doing what is 'right' but must incorporate reflections on the values of people who use services, staff and the organization. What are the ethical dilemmas and what are the tensions?

2. **Person-centred practice:** The MCA places the person at the centre of decision-making. The MCA does not just apply to people who lack capacity (hence why it is not called the Mental Incapacity Act) but is about how capacity is maximized and how we support people to make decisions).

3. **Legal and policy requirements:** Standards need to be met. The CQC will inspect the care you offer and organizations want to ensure they offer the best possible care to those in their charge, not because the CQC demand this, but because basic principles of humanity tells us this is the right thing to do. Law and policy combines to provide requirements and guidance on what needs to be done, but most importantly, why doing it according to these guidelines actually may make life easier for services and essentially people who use those services.

By combining these three factors and working with staff to discuss the MCA, and by using this book to help you work through some of the dilemmas in practice, it is hoped that the culture of care that the MCA represents can be experienced in practice by all involved in the process of delivering and receiving care.

Robert Francis in his report made reference to the warning signs of problematic cultures of care. This is a non-exhaustive list but includes:

- patient stories

- mortality

- complaints

- staff concerns
- whistleblowers
- governance
- finance
- staff reductions.

There is a fear around disclosing information that might shine a light on abusive cultures of care because of fear of reprisal, but the message of this book is for people who use services, practitioners and family members to reflect upon how legislation helps them to stand up for people's rights and provide best care. It's what the MCA says, not what you say – so that in itself can be helpful to you in locating your concern within the supportive framework of legislation.

This will become much clearer as we draw together messages and themes as we proceed through this book.

Chapter 2

Maximizing Capacity

Before we begin with this chapter, we must remind ourselves of the first principle of the Act:

A person must be assumed to have capacity unless it is established that he lacks capacity.

This principle makes clear that making decisions on behalf of another person or even commencing a capacity assessment must begin with a reason to believe that the person may lack capacity. It also underlines the fact that people have the right to make their own decisions – unless it is established that they lack capacity to make the specific decision at hand. So what has occurred that has led you to believe that the individual concerned is unable to make his or her own decision?

The Care Act 2014 (at the time of writing, Part I of the Act will be implemented in April 2015, while other parts will come into force later) has a focus on providing support to people when they have 'substantial difficulty' in being involved in specific decisions.

Substantial difficulty in one or more of the following:

1. Understanding relevant information.
2. Retaining that information.
3. Using or weighing that information as part of the process.
4. Communicating their views, wishes or feelings.

This involves identifying what these difficulties are and then addressing them through providing appropriate support such as advocacy, or another person in their lives. It may be that the person with support is then able to make his or her own decisions or it may transpire that the person lacks capacity and a best interests decision then needs to be made under the Mental Capacity Act. It could be argued that this element is no different from the Mental Capacity Act, namely, there must be an identification of how and why the person may be unable (or have difficulties) in making their own decisions, and then support provided to enable decision-making or decision-making involvement. All of this must occur *before*, where applicable, decisions are made on their behalf.

So before beginning any assessment of capacity:

1. What is the decision that needs to be made?

2. What problems or difficulties is the person having relating to this decision?

3. What support do they need?

Communication and choice

One key element within this process is communication:

- Does the person understand why the subject has been raised about the situation they are currently experiencing?

- Do they understand what the decision is and why this decision (or proposal) is being raised in the first place?

- Has there been a discussion about the presenting issue with the person?

- Is the person able to convey his or her own understanding of the options surrounding the current issue?

- How much has been communicated or is known about the person's presentation or personality before there was a query about capacity?

- Has the process for best interests decision-making, where there are concerns about someone's ability to make decisions been explained to the person? And do they understand this?

Without exploring the above, there is a risk that a presumption of *incapacity* is what starts the process and an immediate move towards considering best interests decision-making takes place. This is not the intention of the Act.

Triggers for assessment

Whilst the capacity test (to be covered later on in the book) begins with the diagnostic element, a diagnosis in itself is not a reason to query capacity. The Act makes this clear; we cannot assume that because a person has dementia, a mental disorder, brain injury or learning disability that their decision-making abilities are not present. It may, however, be that a person's diagnosis is the reason that capacity has been queried – for example, a person's behaviour has changed since an acquired brain injury, or their actions since an event that caused their impairment are not in line with their usual decision-making. So it is (usually) their actions, change in communication or behaviour rather than simply a 'label' they have, that flag up the query.

The following is based on a real-life case and whilst it relates to a decision about accommodation, it highlights some significant factors relating to communication and understanding what affects a person's capacity.

Case study: Communicating relevant and need-to-know information

Joe is in a brain injury rehab unit following a motorbike accident. A decision needs to be made about his discharge/follow-on care. Joe's view is that he wants to return to live his life as it was in the community. Joe is estranged from his wife, but the staff on the unit feels she is the most appropriate person to consult with because she is related to Joe despite the fact that Joe himself says he wants his best friend Mike to advocate and speak on his behalf. Neither Mike nor Joe understand why he can't discharge himself and whilst they understand he needs further rehab, they are confused as to why the decision needs to be made by someone else. They keep being told that Joe lacks capacity, but Mike feels he has capacity as he can express a view. This has led to both parties feeling that they are being excluded from the decision-making process.

It is important to remember that everyone responds to new situations differently, particularly if they don't understand why the decision is being discussed. Communication is key from the outset and understanding the person's background, including any significant life events must be explored as far as possible.

What happened	What should have happened
Staff had not explained the MCA or how decisions needed to be made to anyone other than Joe's wife.	To enable all those in Joe's life to have a role in best interests decision-making it was important that they all understood the framework professionals were using.
An explanation of what capacity means had not been explained to Joe or Mike, therefore leaving them with the view that capacity equated to expressing a view.	Clarification as to what the capacity test was needed to be communicated to all, including Joe.
By only consulting with Joe's wife, who offered a negative view about Mike, a decision was made that Mike was inappropriate to consult with, and he was taken out of best interests decision-making despite Joe's wishes to the contrary.	All parties interested in the welfare of Joe should have been consulted in order to form a full picture about Joe, his life and what was important. Placing more weight on a person's view purely because of their relationship with the person potentially provides an inaccurate portrayal of Joe and factors relating to the decision.
Joe's lifestyle and personality were not factored into the way he expressed himself (at times it appeared he was verbally abusive to staff and aggressive) and his way of communicating was put down to his brain injury.	Information should have been gathered from others who experienced Joe in different environments and could report on how he actually behaved when in the company of others. This information highlighted that this was the way he had always talked and behaved when with friends or in environments that weren't 'home', which was quite different.

In this example it was Joe's brain injury and presumptions made because of it that led others to believe he lacked capacity and it was this that led the decision-making process, which in turn began to exclude Joe himself from it. That is not to say that there were not grounds for querying his capacity, but that by presuming incapacity it changed communication and involvement. Shifting the focus to maximizing capacity through the provision of support could not only ensure Joe was fully involved in the decision, but could also open up transparent communication to improve any potential best interests decision-making.

There is therefore a need to identify the reason for querying a person's capacity and consider the range of communication provision available. This is done by:

- Providing information on the options, benefits and risks associated.

- Consulting with the person's family, friends and carers.

- Considering cultural aspects and their influence on the person, the decision-making, their communication or presentation.

- Considering the individual's preferences, for example, time of day, environment, decisional-supports (such as people who have been identified as important to the person).

- Considering effects of medication and treatment.

- Exploring different ways of communicating.

- Taking into account the person's circumstances.

Provide support

Once it has been identified why there is a belief that a person may lack capacity to make a decision, it is then important to consider Principle 2 of the Mental Capacity Act:

A person is not to be treated as unable to make a decision unless all practicable steps to help him to do so have been taken without success.

Key questions to consider at this stage are:

1. What support can be offered to enable someone to make their own decisions?

2. What is affecting the person's understanding, retention of information, weighing up and using the information and/or communicating it? How can this be addressed?

3. Can information be provided in an easy-read format, through pictures or words? Which works best for the person?

4. Are there others in the person's life that can support the person on the decision at hand, a family member, advocate, friend or member of staff they get on well with?

5. Is language or communication a factor that needs to be addressed?

Recognize the differing needs of clients

Whilst an assessment of capacity must be as person-centred as possible, there will be client groups who have particular needs or difficulties that mean it is evident that they will be unable to make their own decisions in this area. However, the process of supported decision-making is still an important one, if only to be considered and then disregarded, if there is clear evidence that the person lacks capacity. Whilst this chapter focuses on maximizing and supporting decision-making, it is not suggesting that this is possible for all people, but rather that consideration must be given to supported decision-making and identifying where it has been difficult or in some cases impossible.

Table 2.1: The differing needs of clients

Client need	Impact on capacity
Neurological impairment from birth	The person's impairment means they may have been unable to understand or carry out certain decisions all their life.
Person not in contact with services prior to impairment	The person is not known to services until the cause for their lacking capacity arises (for example, as a result of a brain injury or stroke) or at such an advanced stage (such as dementia) when contact with services occurs and the ability to learn or retain new information has passed.
Impairment is in an advanced stage with regards to ability to make decisions	Similar to the above situation and where the person has not made any preparations for future decisions about themselves.

cont.

Client need	Impact on capacity
The person is in a coma, vegetative or minimally conscious state	Where someone is unconscious or unaware (such as someone in a coma or vegetative state) the nature of the person's brain injury and subsequent diagnosis give a clear indication of their lacking capacity. A person in a minimally conscious state may still be deemed to lack capacity, but may be able to express a view (as opposed to make a decision).

What is important to consider, whoever the person is and whatever their disability, difficulty or need is, is that they must be treated as individuals in a person-centred way; the element of supported decision-making is one that flows through the Mental Capacity Act. The key is identifying exactly what support a person may need or benefit from.

Provide all relevant information and support

People rarely make decisions in isolation; therefore it would be unreasonable to assume that where a person is having difficulty in making a decision, they are unable to or lack the capacity to do so. Most people need support to make decisions and will be unable to make informed choices without the appropriate information, opportunity to discuss this and to be afforded the time. This is no different when working with people within the framework of the Act.

In the following Court of Protection Judgement we see a very useful summary from Baker J with regards to assessing capacity, making best interests decisions and the element of full exploration of these with the person.

Case study: CC v KK and STCC EWHC 2136 (COP)

KK was an 83-year-old woman with a diagnosis of Parkinson's disease and vascular dementia. KK's husband died whilst KK was in her early 70s, and she moved to a small village into a rented bungalow. Due to her physical health she had been in contact with social services for some time and in 2010 was admitted to hospital following a fall at home.

Whilst in hospital she presented as confused and muddled and was assessed as lacking capacity; a proposal (and later best interests decision) was made for her to be discharged into a residential care home. A short time later she was assessed as having capacity following some improvement and returned home. Over a period of months her physical health deteriorated and she was later assessed as lacking capacity and was admitted to a nursing home where a deprivation of liberty authorization was put in place, which was challenged by KK herself who wanted to be at home, and it is this that led to the case being heard in the Court of Protection.[1]

> There is, I perceive, a danger that professionals, including judges, may objectively conflate a capacity assessment with a best interests analysis and conclude that the person under review should attach greater weight to the physical security and comfort of a residential home and less importance to the emotional security and comfort that the person derives from being in their own home. I remind myself again of the danger of the 'protection imperative' identified by Ryder J in Oldham MBC v GW and PW (supra). These considerations underpin the cardinal rule, enshrined in statute, that a person is not to be treated as unable to make a decision merely because she makes what is perceived as being an unwise one.
>
> Para 68: Capacity assessors should not start with a blank canvas: 'The person under evaluation must be presented with detailed options so that their capacity to weigh up those options can be fairly assessed.'
>
> Para 67: In this case, I perceive a real danger that in assessing KK's capacity professionals and the court may consciously or subconsciously attach excessive weight to their own views of how her physical safety may be best protected and insufficient weight to her own views of how her emotional needs may best be met.
>
> Para 68. This danger is linked, in my view, to a further problem with the local authority's approach in this case... I find that the local authority has not identified a complete package of support that would or might be available should KK return home, and that this has undermined the experts' assessment of her capacity.
>
> The statute requires that, before a person can be treated as lacking capacity to make a decision, it must be shown that all practicable steps have been taken to help her to do so.
>
> As the Code of Practice makes clear, each person whose capacity is under scrutiny must be given 'relevant information' including 'what the likely consequences of

---

1   Baker J's summary follows – for the full judgement go to www.bailii.org/ew/
     cases/EWHC/COP/2012/2136.html, accessed 2 December 2014.

a decision would be (the possible effects of deciding one way or another).' That requires a detailed analysis of the effects of the decision either way, which in turn necessitates identifying the best ways in which option would be supported.

In order to understand the likely consequences of deciding to return home, KK should be given full details of the care package that would or might be available. The choice which KK should be asked to weigh up is not between the nursing home and a return to the bungalow with no or limited support, but rather between staying in the nursing home and a return home with all practicable support. I am not satisfied that KK was given full details of all practicable support that would or might be available should she return home to her bungalow.

Para 69. When considering KK's capacity to weigh up the options for her future residence, I adopt the approach of Macur J in LBJ v RYJ (supra), namely that it is not necessary for a person to demonstrate a capacity to understand and weigh up every detail of the respective options, but merely the salient factors. In this case, KK may lack the capacity to understand and weigh up every nuance or detail. In my judgement, however, she does understand the salient features, and I do not agree that her understanding is 'superficial.'

She understands that she needs carers four times a day and is dependent on them for supporting all activities in daily living. She understands that she needs to eat and drink, although she has views about what she likes and dislikes, and sometimes needs to be prompted. She understands that she may be lonely at home and that it would not be appropriate to use the lifeline merely to have a chat with someone. She understands that if she is on her own at night there may be a greater risk to her physical safety.

Whilst this judgement on some level reiterates the Act and what both Principles 1 and 2 state, it is important to reflect on the fact that much of the decision-making occurred without the Court's involvement and only went to Court because the person themselves was objecting. This judgement should make clear that the Act is applicable regardless of where that decision-making is occurring and that a full exploration of the relevant factors must be carried out, communicated with the person and in particular identifying what support may be required for any of these elements.

Decision-makers and all those involved in best interests decision-making should consider:

- What support does the person need to help them make a decision?

- Do they have all the information in a format that suits them?

- Considering the options available, has the person been offered full opportunity to digest the information about each one?

- Are there different levels of support available? For example, if it's a decision between a care home or returning home, what type of support can be offered at home as oppose to a care home? Has this been fully communicated? Merely stating that one option will have staff there all the time and the other one won't does not give the person a clear understanding or expectation of what this means in reality.

- Is what is considered 'best' for them leading the decision making process and potentially disregarding their capacitated views or choices?

Try to understand the person's situation

It is imperative that individuals are treated with understanding and empathy when what can often be a life-changing decision is being proposed. Without this a person may feel unable to fully discuss or share their views, wishes or feelings. Even the language used when describing the person or their situation is an important issue to be considered. For example, describing a person as presenting with 'challenging or difficult behaviour' does not usually convey what their experience actually is. They may be frightened or confused, or need others to speak to them calmly and provide reassurance. Describing them as challenging merely seeks to reinforce a culture of care that is not supportive of their situation or acknowledging how it feels for them and unintentionally excludes them from being involved.

Case study

Serena is in hospital having suffered a major brain haemorrhage 2 weeks previously. She has been left without movement on her left side, though is beginning to regain some movement in her left leg. Serena has three young children at home, a husband and an extended family. The family own three corner shops including a takeaway. Serena states that because of this she will be looked after with food as well as care and support from her family given they all work and live so close to each other. The clinical team determines that she is ready for discharge and arranges a meeting to discuss this, which includes the options available to her such as rehab. One of the nurses comments that Serena does not have capacity as she believes that once she returns home she will be able to recuperate with the help and support of her family. The nurse feels she has 'no insight' into her needs and that a best interests decision should be taken.

In this case study, whilst it may transpire in the long term that Serena does not have capacity to make a decision about where she goes on discharge from the hospital, the word 'insight' is not part of assessing a person's capacity and can often be used to describe someone when it actually means that they disagree with another person's view about them.

Serena has experienced a life-changing event and it would be unusual for anyone to experience this type of an event without having hope for the future. It is important to try to understand what the impact has had on a person as well as how it feels when suddenly others are seemingly in a position of making decisions about your life.

Allow time for the person

Considering the examples given so far in this chapter, was there an opportunity to delay the decision-making process? Or rather, how much of an opportunity was there to spend time with the person, provide them with information, explore the options with them, identify others that can support the person?

Best interests decision-making should not be viewed as an isolative process; it is an ongoing one as we saw in *CC v KK and STCC* even when a decision has been made and put into action. It must be remembered that capacity can be an ever-changing progression or regression and factors such as the person's environment, information processing, thought processes, medication, physical health all impact on decision-making and there are numerous variants attached to this:

- context
- what we know and are familiar with
- personal values – even when there's evidence against that
- comparing the past with the present
- external factors
- choice
- weighing up outcomes
- understanding information and options
- emotion
- support from others
- community presence.

All of these, and other factors, form part of individual decision-making and yet there can be a drive towards speedy capacity assessments and decision-making when it comes to best interests. This is despite the fact that it would be fair to say many of us would not make a decision about moving house, changing job, making an expensive purchase or about our own independence (such as an increase in it or loss of it) without due consideration. The Mental Capacity Act is not intended to discriminate against those that lack capacity or who may have difficulty in making a decision, therefore it is vital that this framework is not used unfairly, that is, with an expectation that decision-making is a quick process. The person must be given as much opportunity to enable them to make a decision (where this is possible) or at the very least to be as fully involved as possible.

Open questions
Assessing or identifying the need for support can be enhanced by the way in which questions are posed to the person; this can sometimes allow for a more comprehensive overview as to what the difficulty is that the person is experiencing, what their concerns are or what others can do to help them. So within a conversation aim for open questions such as:

- Can you tell me in your own words what I've just said?

- Can you tell me what your understanding is of option A and then of option B?

- Can you explain why you think this is being discussed with you?

- What for you is better (or worse) about option A or option B?

- What is important for you about this decision that you want others to know and why?

Environment and timing

It is not only the environment as to where the person is at the time of requiring support in decision-making, but also where the environment is part of the decision-making process. Again, thinking about our own lives, we wouldn't move to another area or house without visiting it first. Supporting someone in visiting a prospective care home, taking pictures of the home or staff, images of the area and identifying what is in the local area that is important to the person should all form part of maximizing capacity.

Similarly a change in environment may impact on a person's ability to make a decision. For example, a person with dementia may feel confused on admission to hospital because it is an unknown environment. It may be difficult to strike up any relationship with staff because the person bringing medication changes each time adding to their confusion, or the person is moved from ward to ward because of a change in their medical needs. These slight changes must not be underestimated or assumed as a clear indicator about a person's lack of capacity.

- Is there an opportunity for only one or two people to discuss the decision with them so that they don't feel overwhelmed or under pressure?

- Is there an opportunity to meet with the person in a different environment that they are more familiar with, for example, escorting them home for the day?

- Can the decision be discussed with them in their normal environment? For example, a decision about medical treatment may be discussed in the hospital at an outpatient appointment or pre-(medical) assessment appointment. But have they felt able to or had time to process relevant information/ask questions in these situations? Or with time and an alternative environment would they then feel in more of a position to discuss the decision?

A change in the person's usual environment can make them feel vulnerable or disempowered, particularly where that environment is one where they are receiving care, treatment or support (such as a hospital or care home) or where others are in a position of power. Whilst it may not be possible to change the environment, it is a factor that should be considered.

Values

Principle 3 of the Act reinforces an important element of the law, that is that we all have the right to make our own decisions where we have the capacity to do so. Often our decisions are influenced by our own values-based system. This is influenced by many factors including our childhoods, family, life experiences, profession, environment, religion, culture and so on.

Principle 3: *'A person is not to be treated as unable to make a decision merely because he makes an unwise decision.'*

Everybody has their own values, beliefs, preferences and attitudes. A person should not be assumed to lack the capacity to make a decision just because other people think their decision is unwise. This applies even if family members, friends or healthcare or social care staff are unhappy with a decision.

There is a risk as the above illustrates that where a person's values are incompatible with decision-makers or those of the environment they are in, that they are deemed to lack capacity. For example, a care home may have certain policies that do not fit with a person's values or what is important to them.

Case study
John has terminal cancer and most recently has been diagnosed with early onset dementia. As part of a best interests decision he was moved into a hospice one week ago. At the time he was very unwell, unable to communicate and was sedated most of

the day. Since the move, his physical health has improved and he is able to make most decisions on his own. It is recognized that he has possibly only weeks to live. At present his only nutrition and hydration is via a percutaneous endoscopic gastrostomy (PEG), and John wishes for this to be removed as he states he does not wish to prolong his life any longer and accepts he is reaching the end of his life. A Priest from the Catholic church founded the hospice and it retains its religious foundations although faith is not a pre-requisite for admission. A member of the board of trustees hears about John's decision and informs staff that they must carry out a capacity assessment. He cannot accept that someone of 'sound mind' would effectively end their life, which is how he views this, and believes a best interests decision must be made that ensures John's life comes to a natural end. John, however, reiterates that he has watched many members of his family die from cancer and that it is his choice to end treatment.

In this example John's values are in contradiction with that of the hospice as well as some of the staff that are part of everyday decision-making. They are used to working with people who are at the end of their life, but have not been part of what they feel is supporting a person to end their life.

Where it is evident that either a decision-maker's own values or those of where they are residing/receiving care are incompatible, this information must be communicated and be open and transparent, and not a driver towards a preferred outcome.

Professionals, family or friends will likely have their own values that may be so enshrined in who they are they become the driving force in decision-making.

Examples of where values may influence decisions

Care Home Sunlight provides accommodation for adults over the age of 65. It is common practice for everyone to have the flu jab; where a person is unable to consent, a best interests decision is made for the person to receive this.

In this example, has consideration been given to the individual's own values; would they choose to have a recommended vaccination if they had capacity? Whilst the health benefits should be considered in making the best interests decision, there is a risk that others' values in terms of medicine unduly influence the decision. Some people actively choose because of their own values not to take medication or to have vaccinations, and this must be factored into the decision-making process.

> David has a mental disorder and lives in supported accommodation. His diet is particularly unhealthy and he likes to spend his money on takeaway food and snacks. It is assessed that he lacks the capacity to fully understand the health risks associated with his diet and a best interests decision is taken in order to control the amount of money he has on a daily basis, which in turn will limit the available funds for purchasing food.

In this example, others' values about what is 'best' for David may influence the outcome of a capacity assessment. Many people make unwise decisions about their diet (or are viewed by others as unwise). All steps must be taken to determine whether this is a choice by David as well as ensuring that the bar set for assessing capacity is not higher than for someone who does not have an impairment and therefore would not have their capacity assessed.

> Beverley has a learning disability and spends £20 of her weekly benefits on scratch cards. The local authority feel they are endorsing gambling by allowing this to occur and seek to hold a best interests meeting to discuss whether she has the capacity to continue doing this.

In this example a best interests meeting is held before Beverley's capacity has even been assessed and as a result places what may be an unwise decision into the framework of the Act without due consideration as to why capacity is being queried. Where there are concerns for an element of a person's decision-making, it must not be assumed that they lack capacity when there has been no communication with the person about these concerns or a demonstration that support can be provided where necessary.

Independence and autonomy

The concept of autonomy has become an important one both within health and social care decision-making as well as within the courts. What has also become particularly important is that even when a person may be viewed as lacking capacity, that there is still a framework in place that recognizes the importance of individuals being provided with full support to make their own decisions.

Definition of autonomy *(Collins English Dictionary)*

1. The right or state of self-government, especially when limited.

2. A state, community, or individual possessing autonomy.

3. Freedom to determine one's own actions, behaviour, etc.

(*Philosophy*)

4. The doctrine that the individual human will is or ought to be governed only by its own principles and laws.

5. The state in which one's actions are autonomous.

The following case considered where others may view a person as lacking capacity because of their 'unwise' decision-making, but which was in fact someone making autonomous decisions.

Case study: Wandsworth CCG v IA and TA (2014)

IA suffered a violent assault and sustained a serious head injury in 2007. He had suffered from numerous problems following this that included poor memory, inflexibility of thought, impulsivity and mood control. Following an emergency admission to hospital related to his diabetes, he reached the point of being ready for discharge and it was this decision that went to court to determine his capacity.[2]

> Para 67: I am of the view that IA does have the capacity to make decisions about his medical treatment, future residential care, and property and financial affairs, and I shall so declare.
>
> Para 68: It seems to me that it has been of considerable benefit to IA that practical steps have been taken (including careful explanation by a trusted professional, Dr. Bashir) to assist him to reach these decisions, weighing up the information relevant to that decision; I trust that such assistance will be available to him in the future.
>
> Para 69: Although I am of the view that IA has made a number of unwise decisions in the past about his medical treatment and home living conditions, these
>
> 1. are not demonstrative of lack of capacity;
>
> 2. are more reflective of his somewhat challenging personality; and

---

2 The full details of this case can be found in the judgement available at www.bailii. org/ew/cases/EWHC/COP/2014/990.html, accessed 2 December 2014, but it is the summary from Cobb J that is of use in explaining elements of the principles of independence and autonomy.

3. in some respects in any event ante-date his acute brain injury and could not therefore be attributable to acquired cognitive deficit. Moreover, there is reason to believe that his resistance to social work intervention is probably founded in a long-standing grievance about the compulsory purchase of his home, exacerbated by his suspicions about the plans of the authority for his future care.

Full consideration must be given to what leads some people to make certain decisions in their life. Maximizing support must not be something that is provided or carried out in order to simply reach a conclusion that the person lacks capacity. It must be part of a culture of care. How a person has historically made decisions in their life, how they may or may not have previously accepted support must be taken into account as well as whether autonomy is a concept that's important to them. Some people may have never had the opportunity to make their own decisions because others have always done this for them; this may be the norm for them and a preference in itself. Alternatively they may not have the skills to make their own decisions but with support could do so.

Much of the above can also be considered with regards to a person's independence and in particular how support can be offered to ensure a person maintains as much independence as possible. As stated earlier in this chapter, often the person who is at the heart of decision-making under the Act will be experiencing a life-changing event where the following factors may apply:

- a reduced level or opportunity to make choices

- a loss of physical independence

- adjusting to a disability or diagnosis

- presence in the community

- mental, emotional and overall wellbeing

- becoming dependent on others for care

- recognising their own difficulties in decision-making

- a sense or actual experience of being disempowered

- loss or bereavement.

This list is not exhaustive and care must be taken in ensuring that when there are discussions about forthcoming decisions with the person that these are acknowledged and factored in as to how the person may communicate. Being able to own these feelings or share them may be the only way the person feels they have some level of control.

Table 2.2: Maximizing capacity and supported decision-making – checklist

Identify the decision that needs to be made.	
What is the information that is actually relevant to the decision?	
What problems or difficulties is the person having with regards to this decision?	
What support does the person need to help them make a decision?	
Does the person understand why the subject has been raised about the situation they are currently experiencing?	
Is the person able to convey his or her own understanding of the options surrounding the current issue?	
How much has been communicated or is known about the person's presentation or personality before there was a query about capacity?	
Do they have all the information in a format that suits them?	
Considering the options available, has the person been offered a full opportunity to digest the information about each one?	
Has there been consideration given to the person's culture and its influence on the person, the decision-making, their communication or presentation?	
Has consideration been given to the individual's preferences, e.g. time of day, environment, decisional supports?	
Identify where possible what a person's decisional supports are – friends, family, environment, information from external sources, e.g. the internet, specific websites.	

Identify others in the person's life that may offer an insight into the person's life, for example, in situations where the person is unable to describe themselves in order to provide a full picture as to how they usually make decisions.	
Are you able to explore different ways of communicating?	
Would the person benefit from an independent advocate, someone that is not directly involved in the decision-making process, but is there only for the person?	
Consider the use of scenarios or props in discussing the decision at hand, the options available or the possible outcomes related to these.	
Take into account the person's circumstances.	
Take care in not assuming that because a person expresses different views to those of decision-makers that they lack capacity; rather explore this with the person and be open to their point of view and perspective.	
Consider issues of autonomy and independence.	

Chapter 3

Assessing Capacity

The previous chapter discussed maximizing capacity, as it is important that maximizing capacity is considered prior to assessing capacity. There is a very clear reason for this, and that is that we should not just launch into assessing someone's capacity because we are told to do so, because we think that the MCA says so or because we make an assumption based upon someone's appearance, diagnosis or perception of disability. Supporting someone to make a decision by maximizing his or her capacity should be a central tenet to MCA inspired good practice. A question that you could ask yourself is this:

> *'What right do I have to assess this person's capacity and why would I even do so?'*

This might seem a rather obscure question to ask, but it is a question that starts off the principle of considering why we would even assess capacity. It would be very easy and perhaps quite natural to start off a chapter on assessing capacity by writing about how to assess capacity and by looking at what the MCA states about assessing capacity, but this book is about the spirit of the Act and about emancipatory practice (which has been discussed earlier). By looking at the above question we start to consider the concept of *power* (as in how powerful assessing someone's capacity can be, particularly if the determination is that the person lacks capacity) because to hold the keys to making a decision that someone lacks capacity is a powerful act. It is thinking about it in this way that results in many practitioners feeling somewhat anxious about ever wanting to assess capacity.

But let's break this down somewhat rather than viewing assessing capacity as this big task that you might do with an equally big decision being made.

You are always assessing capacity – whether you know it or not!

As we have already considered in previous chapters and will continue to reflect upon in this book, capacity is decision-specific and time-specific, so let's lose this myth that is in practice about 'people lacking mental capacity'. If you hear someone referring to an individual as lacking capacity, say, for example, a doctor, nurse or social worker, it is important that you consider this statement critically as it is fairly commonplace to read in notes and hear professionals and carers refer to a person who 'lacks capacity'. So, in being critical, ask two questions.

1. What for?

2. What evidence do you have?

This might sound somewhat defensive and a little provocative to ask, but the intention is not to do that, but rather to explore whether the MCA is being applied in practice. Capacity should not be considered outside the realms of the MCA and, certainly, capacity should not be assessed in any other context than how the MCA instructs us to assess capacity. Mental capacity is decision-specific and time-specific, and it's not common to encounter anyone who will ever lack capacity *per se* to make all decisions. If the person who states 'lacks capacity' is unable to state what decision they believe P is unable to make, or what evidence they have to substantiate that claim, then the assumption of capacity must be considered to stand and the person has capacity. The MCA is very clear when is states that P must be assumed to have capacity unless it is established that he lacks capacity (S1(1)). If there is no evidence of this being established, then the assumption of capacity is there.

In practice and when carers in home settings are supporting vulnerable adults, capacity is always being assessed – as said previously, you just don't know you are doing it!

Case study

Harvey decides he wants to make a cup of tea in the care home he lives in. He goes into the kitchen and boils the kettle and proceeds to make his cup of tea. Sandra, a member of staff who observes this, goes into the kitchen and asks Harvey if she can help him whilst she takes the kettle and supports him to fill the mug. The cup of tea is made and Harvey enjoys it.

There is nothing complicated about the above transaction between Harvey and Sandra. This is very straightforward but unbeknownst to Sandra, she has just applied sections 1, 2, 3 and 4 of the MCA.

Section 1: Sandra reflected and has clearly applied the five principles of the Act. She has assumed his capacity, supported his decision-making and most certainly used the least restrictive option when deciding how to support him.

Sections 2 and 3: Assessing capacity. We will come to this shortly and you will be able to see how Sandra applied them.

Section 4: Best interests (see Chapter 6). Sandra most certainly supported Harvey in upholding his best interests. More about this later.

Before we proceed with how capacity is assessed, let's remind ourselves of what the code of practice tells us.

An assessment of a person's capacity must be based on their ability to make a specific decision at the time it needs to be made, and not their ability to make decisions in general. (CoP 4.4)

This point was made (above) but it is important to know what specific decision we might be assessing the person to make. In the above scenario the decision that Sandra was assessing Harvey's capacity in relation to was him making a cup of tea, particularly around whether he could understand the risks involved in using a kettle with boiling hot water inside. Admittedly, Sandra may not have considered herself to be assessing Harvey's capacity – but she was. It was this 'assessment' that actually propelled her to go into the kitchen and intervene, albeit that the intervention was highly supportive and not restrictive upon Harvey's independence at all.

As mentioned in Chapter 6, it is suggested that we can break down decisions that people make into two broad categories – less complex and complex decisions. The rule of thumb when considering what these decisions might look like can be considered as follows:

- **Less complex** – day-to-day decisions such as what you eat, drink, wear. Where you might shop and how and when you might access primary care for routine medical appointments such as the GP, dentist or optician.

- ○ These decisions may not require a record of assessment of capacity and can be made as and when required with minimal intervention required on the part of the practitioner, but staff must still be able to justify their decisions, actions and provide an evidence base. Sandra will be able to justify this quite easily in relation to Harvey and how she knows that making a cup of tea can be difficult for him due to his learning disability.

- **Complex** – decisions that require greater consideration in relation to serious medical treatment, change of residence or spending of large amounts of money.

- ○ These decisions will require a robust assessment that might need to be planned, clearly not the case in an emergency, but will require recording, consultation with others, perhaps a best interests meeting and, possibly, consultation with a Lasting Power of Attorney or the Court of Protection (see Chapter 5).

Regardless of whether the decision made is less complex or more complex, the assessment of capacity follows exactly the same process. So, essentially, a Judge in the Court or Protection when deciding what might be in P's best interests in relation to serious medical treatment will follow the same guidelines as Sandra will follow when assessing Harvey's capacity to make a cup of tea. These guidelines are the MCA, most notably sections 2 and 3.

The mental capacity test

The MCA is clear that anyone can assess mental capacity, for the very simple reason that they might have to. Assessing capacity is not the domain of the medical profession, including psychiatrists, because assessing capacity is not a medical procedure, even though it might be the case that a doctor needs to assess capacity because the decision in question is in relation to a medical procedure. It's given that the person most involved and knowledgeable about the outcome of that decision should ideally be the person assessing the person's capacity.

It is a myth to suggest that only psychiatrists assess capacity or that care managers should be from the local authority. If you consider that it is likely to be you assessing P's capacity because it is you delivering the care or treatment, then this will make the process less cumbersome and certainly less bureaucratic, but do ask, *'Who is the person most likely to be involved in following this decision through?'* If the assessment of capacity is in relation to an older person who is considered to require residential care when they leave hospital, then if a care manager is involved they, having fully consulted where possible with relatives and hospital professionals, should be undertaking the capacity assessment. This is because it is likely to be them who will be instrumental in the process of seeking the care home.

Sections 2 and 3 of the MCA are where we find the *two stage* mental capacity assessment. Basically, you assess mental capacity by asking questions to yourself and then seeking, through assessment, answers to those questions.

Stage one

Does the person have an impairment of, or disturbance in the functioning of, the mind or brain?

The MCA states that it does not matter whether the impairment or disturbance is permanent or temporary.

This question generates much anxiety amongst carers and those who perceive themselves to be non-medically trained (what being medically trained has ever had to do with it, no-one is really sure!). Many carers will ask themselves what they know about impairments or disturbances in the functioning of the mind or brain, but with respect to our colleagues in care homes and hospitals it might be a case that they are reading the question wrongly. The question is *not* asking whether the person has a learning disability, dementia, brain injury, or any other disability or ailment for that matter. It is simply asking what it is asking. We do not have X-ray machines readily available to really tell us at any given time what someone's impairment or disturbance might be, so this is not a scientific question that necessitates a scientific response. The MCA asks for us to have a *reasonable belief on the balance of probabilities* that there is sufficient evidence to suggest an impairment or disturbance. The following could apply:

- **Impairment:** A diagnosed mental illness, including dementia, learning disability, brain injury or organic difficulty such as a brain tumour.

- **Disturbance:** Being intoxicated through alcohol or drugs, having a urine infection leading to impaired thinking, confusion, diabetes causing blood sugar levels to affect capacity, infections (such as chest infections).

These lists are non-exhaustive and are not intending to be prescriptive, but do give the reader an insight into how to make a judgement in relation to a reasonable belief on the balance of probabilities (which effectively means that it is more likely than not) that P has an impairment or disturbance in the functioning of the mind or brain.

If the answer to this question is *no*, then that is the end of the mental capacity assessment as the person has the mental capacity to be able to make a decision for themselves. This tells us that merely being unable to make a decision is not necessarily an indication of a lack of mental capacity; the inability to make a decision *must* be based upon an impairment or disturbance in the functioning of the mind or brain, as outlined above.

If, however, the answer to this question is *yes* then you will proceed to stage two of the assessment, which is still found in section 2 of the MCA.

Stage two
Is the impairment or disturbance sufficient to cause the person to be unable to make that particular decision at the relevant time?
At this point carers may ask how they could possibly know this; well, the MCA tells us by offering section 3, which looks at the four parts of decision-making.

The MCA states that a person is unable to make a particular decision if they cannot do one or more of the following four things:

1. Can the person understand information given to them?
This extends beyond the realms of spoken English as all efforts should be made, including interpreters if necessary, to enable the

person to understand information, but concepts of comprehension and someone being able or not able to grasp what is being said to them must be considered here. Chapter 4.16 of the Code of Practice refers to relevant information in determining if P can understand information relating to:

- the nature of the decision
- the reason why the decision is needed, and
- the likely effects of deciding one way or another, or making no decision at all.

Section 3(2) of the MCA makes it clear that information must be presented in a way that is appropriate for that person. The individual assessing capacity will need to reflect upon this and decide how information is presented in order to maximize capacity.

*2. Can that person retain that information long
enough to be able to make a decision?*
This is where the assessor will take into consideration someone's memory, probably short-term more than long-term, and will need to seek information from others in relation to what P's memory is like. It is important to remember that people who can only retain information for a short time must not automatically be assumed to lack capacity. Context is important in how someone's retention of information might be a determinant in their not having capacity.

*3. Can the person use or weigh up the information
available to make the decision?*
This is different to whether someone can understand information and is more about how P might use this the information in evaluating or how they make up their mind. For example, P may well be able to understand information given to them in relation to a particular decision, but may been unable to assess risk or comprehend the potential outcome of the decision they are making.

4. Can the person communicate their decision?
The person assessing capacity must remain mindful that communication extends beyond verbal speech. S3(1)(d) of the MCA makes an important point about *'talking, sign language or any*

other means.' People might be unable to verbally communicate for a number of reasons, such as unconsciousness or being in a coma, but it is important that the person assessing capacity consults with others and seeks all opportunities to maximize P's communication. Section 2 of the MCA informs us that it does not matter whether the impairment or disturbance is permanent or temporary and fluctuating capacity is important to consider. All of us experience fluctuating capacity to one degree or another at any given time. Tiredness, the environment you are in or feeling unwell all have an impact on our capacity and what we can understand, so it is important to get an overall sense of P's capacity before making a determination of any lack of capacity.

Tip: A starting point for assessing capacity is by looking for inabilities that someone may have to complete a task or to make a *decision*. If inabilities are present, then ask whether they can be explained by the impairment in the functioning of the mind or brain and then decide whether or not to proceed to assessing capacity.

If after asking yourself whether the person has an impairment in the functioning of the mind or brain, you have answered *yes* to *one or more* of the above four questions, based upon P's ability to make a specific decision at a specific time, then you are making a determination that P lacks the mental capacity to make that decision at that time. It is absolutely crucial, however, that the person's inability to make the decision is because of their impairment or disturbance of the mind or brain.

One key judgement from the Court of Protection focused on this very issue. Simply having a mental disorder or any other impairment of the functioning of the mind or brain does not equate lacking capacity and as such the diagnostic element must not be used to shoehorn people into being classed as lacking capacity because of one.

PC and NC v City of York Council [2013] EWCA Civ 478

This case looked at whether PC, a 48-year-old married woman with a diagnosed learning disability, had the capacity to decide whether to live with her husband, NC. This may seem an odd decision to be considering given she was already married to NC but whilst they met in 2001, a year later NC was sentenced to 13 years in prison for serious sexual offences against his previous wives. PC married NC whilst he was in prison in 2006 and NC was released on licence in 2011, which prompted the local authority to consider any safeguarding issues and ultimately PC's capacity to make the decision about living with her husband.

The undisputed facts about the case were that NC was convicted of these offences alongside his father whom he had not had contact with since. NC also denied these offences, which subsequently meant he did not enter into any kind of rehab or therapy programme. There was also no evidence that NC had ever posed a danger to PC or harmed her. Both parties wished to continue their married life living together. PC also accepted NC's version of events in that he had been wrongly convicted.

Hedley J's initial ruling also highlighted the fact that PC clearly had capacity to make a decision about marrying NC in 2006 and nothing had occurred since this time to query her capacity. The local authority also stated that whilst they could not comment on PC's capacity (an assessment that PC lacked capacity was carried out by a consultant psychiatrist), they did believe that were she to feel fearful or at risk from NC that she would communicate this to the local authority. They also felt that the idea of them living apart was 'not tenable' given they were married and wished to live together. The conclusion was that PC lacked capacity but that they should be able to live together under a scheme of monitoring and support provided by the local authority.

The case went to appeal based on the reasoning that the decision by Hedley J was focused on whether PC had the capacity to live with NC (person-specific) rather than whether she had the capacity to decide to live with anyone (act-specific) and that this was not in line with the Act's ethos.

In support of the argument for PC and her capacity, the following points were made (as detailed in the judgement):

1. PC has capacity in every other area of her life, save for the conduct of this litigation;

2. PC had and has retained capacity to marry;

3. PC has extricated herself from unsatisfactory or harmful relationships on two previous occasions;

4. PC has previously lived with NC for a year;

5. The evidence did not support a finding of lack of capacity;

6. There was no other evidence upon which a lack of capacity could be founded.

It was the issue as to how exactly PC lacked capacity that was queried, or rather, whether it had been fully considered that her learning disability had anything to do with her decision making, this became known as the 'causative nexus' and was summarized in the judgement as follows:

> 58. ... There is, however, a danger in structuring the decision by looking to s2(1) primarily as requiring a finding of mental impairment and nothing more and in considering s2(1) first before then going on to look at s3(1) as requiring a finding of inability to make a decision. The danger is that the strength of the causative nexus between mental impairment and inability to decide is watered down. That sequence - 'mental impairment' and then 'inability to make a decision' - is the reverse of that in s2(1) – 'unable to make a decision ... because of an impairment of, or a disturbance in the functioning of, the mind or brain' [emphasis added].
>
> The danger in using s2(1) simply to collect the mental health element is that the key words 'because of' in s2(1) may lose their prominence and be replaced by words such as those deployed by Hedley J: 'referable to' or 'significantly relates to'.

What this means is that the capacity assessment as laid out in the Act asks specifically whether the person lacks capacity because of their impairment. However, there is a risk that practitioners fulfill the diagnostic element of the assessment and never go back to consider whether the person's decision making ability is simply an unwise decision (as viewed by others) or whether it is because of their impairment. The outcome of the appeal was that PC was deemed to have capacity as there was no strong evidence that suggested her learning disability had any influence on decisions she had previously made and was making now.

There is no expectation to recall sections 2 and 3 of the MCA word-for-word, but being mindful of the Act and the requirements that there are for assessing capacity can only serve to enhance better person-centred care and treatment in care homes and hospitals. Here is an easy way to remember the two-stage test for capacity.

How to remember the mental capacity test!

When we think about assessing capacity, let's think about YOU and your ID (because if you are to show it anywhere, it is who you are, you see?).

ID - Stage 1

URUC (you are, you see) - **Stage 2**

ID - impairment or disturbance

U - understand

R - retain

U - use/weigh up

C - communicate

The two stage test for mental capacity!

Routine capacity assessments

There are many examples coming out of practice where people who use services are having their capacity assessed as a matter of course to either meet an inspection requirement, or to ensure that care providers are compliant with the MCA. This is actually a little concerning for several reasons.

Think about yourself for a moment and when you last accessed a health service, bearing in mind that we are all using health services regularly, whether it be seeing our GP, dentist, optician or going to hospital. Ask yourself this question: 'When was my capacity last assessed?' Do you remember being asked any questions that indicated that your capacity was being considered? As discussed earlier, assessments of capacity may occur informally or formally and health professionals obtaining consent to treatment will not always record consent being obtained, unless it involves major treatment and there is a reason why someone's capacity may need to be recorded formally in notes and documents. But on the whole, your capacity will not have been assessed in terms of recording that assessment of capacity and placing that on your notes or records.

So, when care home or hospital staff are asked to undertake routine capacity assessments, the question you need to ask yourself is, why? Is this not actually part of a wider stigmatizing process? Unless this is considered carefully, practitioners can make assumptions that someone's capacity requires consideration on the basis of their age, appearance or any disability which could them propel them into assessing capacity – but principle one of the five principles clearly states that we are to assume someone has capacity unless it has been established otherwise. What, therefore, is propelling practitioners to assess capacity? What are the triggers for assessment?

Triggers for assessment

Staff should always start from a presumption of capacity, then take into account:

- the person's 'behaviour'
- their circumstances
- any concerns raised by other people.

(Ho 2009)

By considering the above it may well be the case that triggers are present. For example, the way P interacts with other or behaves may indicate concerns in relation to capacity. Their circumstances may well also be a trigger for assessment, in that P is in hospital following sustaining a head injury in a car accident and is refusing what is deemed to be necessary treatment. Alternatively, relatives, friends or carers may express opinions that their loved one is acting *'differently'* or *'something isn't right'*. These can all be triggers that might propel us to consider capacity.

But if we assess P's capacity because of these triggers alone, or because P is a vulnerable adult receiving care, then there is tension with the spirit of the MCA. We need to consider *DAD*. If we launch straight into the assessment we're not starting at the beginning of a helpful process. *DAD* stands for:

Decision

What is the decision that is requiring the assessment of capacity? Mental capacity is defined in the Code of Practice chapter 4.1 as the *'ability to make a decision.'* So to assess capacity routinely is not only unnecessary but actually impossible. It makes a farce of the spirit of the Act and turns the MCA from a piece of law that sets out to be emancipatory and supporting to being this piece of routine bureaucracy with the key purpose of defending practitioners in the work they do and to meet standards of care. This is not to say at all that we should not have this in practice, but the primary purpose of the MCA is to defend people's rights to choice, autonomy and self-determination, not to create a being whose capacity we routinely assess.

Assessment

If the decision which you are assessing capacity for, has been established, that is, whether or not Ben who has a learning disability is able to understand the nature of his dental treatment, then you can proceed through the two-stage test for capacity (as outlined above).

Determination

This is the point that can generate some anxiety amongst carers in particular – the question, *'Who am I to determine whether this person lacks capacity or not?'* is often considered, generating some concern. This is not a competence issue but a confidence issue. Nowhere in the MCA does it say you must be sure P lacks capacity or has it (after all the MCA suggests you have capacity unless deemed otherwise); all the MCA requires from the assessor is a reasonable belief that it is more likely than not that P lacks capacity at *this* time to make *that* decision. The best you can do is offer that reasonable belief because it is impossible to do anything else, which is why the MCA requires this, because it can require nothing else.

Thus far in this chapter we have looked at triggers for assessment, that we assess mental capacity according to a decision that may need to be made at a specific time, and the two-stage test for capacity. Later, we shall consider how we record capacity assessments, but first let us consider practice techniques to develop and work on when assessing mental capacity.

It's all about the relationship

Carl Rogers (1902–1987) was one of the most influential psychologists in American history (Kramer 1995). Carl Rogers once said:

> In my early professional years I was asking the question: How can I treat, or cure, or change this person? Now I would phrase the question in this way: How can I provide a relationship which this person may use for his own personal growth? (Rogers 1961)

This statement from the man who brought us client-centred counselling and placed great emphasis upon the relationship between the therapist and the client being of more importance than the work achieved, tells us something of great importance. What it tells us is that the outcome of a mental capacity assessment can be greatly influenced by the person undertaking the assessment of capacity. Placing P at the centre of any assessment and seeing all opportunities to maximize capacity and reassure the individual can ultimately enable the person to empower themselves to put their point across in a way which is meaningful, shows a level of consideration and understanding and supports P to express their wishes, feelings and preferences.

Exercise – marks out of 30!

Reflect upon your own practice and how you feel you interact with those you provide care for. Using a scaling technique, with 1 being poor and 5 being excellent, what score would you give yourself on the following (total minimum of 6 marks, maximum of 30 marks)?

- Ability to engage with P
- Ability to empathize
- Ability to listen
- Warmth
- Respect
- Honesty.

You may wish to keep the marks to yourself or share them with others in a celebratory manner, but what is important is that you (along with your colleagues) can take some time to reflect on the above qualities which are instrumental in conducting a mental capacity assessment, particularly a planned assessment in a hospital or care home environment. We hear stories of people we know visiting health and social care professionals and they will recall positive or negative accounts of their experiences, not necessarily based upon the outcome of the appointment, but often upon how the individual felt, or was made to feel during that appointment.

Engaging with P, empathizing, listening, showing warmth, respect and honesty are not only key skills, but also key values which should be central in the value base of the practitioner, particularly when assessing capacity. The irony is that P's capacity can be affected by an interview that simply does not produce the best from that person because the person conducting the assessment is struggling with use of self in the assessment process. P's potential irritability, anxiety, perception of not listening and not engaging and making comments like, *'Oh, I don't know!'* or *'I can't remember'* can all be viewed as indicators of lacking capacity, but they can actually be indicators of the outcome of an oppressive interview technique that has actually resulted in P responding in that way.

The Code of Practice states that P should not be considered to lack capacity to make a particular decision unless all practicable steps have been taken to provide support to P. When assessing capacity reflect also on how you can support P in the process of the assessment by considering the following:

- Cognitive support – to enable P to understand information about options and consequences.

  ○ This is an opportunity for the person assessing capacity to ask questions and respond in a manner that reflects how P is responding. Reflexive practice (Schön 1983) which means thinking in practice rather than thinking on practice (which is reflective practice) is central in being able to adapt and mirror P and their understanding.

- Communication support – to enable P to express a choice.

  ○ As previously mentioned communicating in a way which is right for P and maximizes P's capacity is a key consideration and all practicable steps must be taken to ensure this happens.

- Environmental support – to maximize P's opportunities to make an autonomous decision.

  ○ Never underestimate the impact that the direct environment around someone can have on their capacity. Noise, privacy, familiar environment, who is present, being comfortable are all considerations to be made when assessing P's capacity. Discussing private matters around the bed area in a hospital can be very unhelpful as P may be reluctant to speak. Thin cotton curtains being pulled around a bed are far from soundproof!

Adapted from Ho (2009)

The MCA in S4(6)(a) states that carers must consider, as far as is reasonably ascertainable, the person's past and present wishes and feelings. Considering the three points above will promote good practice, support P and show compliance with the MCA.

In addition to cognitive, communication and environmental support, there are cultural and demographic factors that ought to be considered when assessing P's capacity. This is to ensure that the person assessing has an awareness of all the circumstances that may have an impact on the outcome of an assessment. This is, of course, a non-exhaustive checklist and may be helpful on planned assessments of capacity, particularly in hospital settings.

Other factors to consider when assessing capacity

Learning difficulties
Consider whether someone is able to take part in your assessment. For example, asking someone to spell a word or do an arithmetic test may be very difficult for them, capacity aside!

Memory
Memory difficulties are not necessarily an indication of lack of capacity. Think about your memory and whether you could remember what is being asked of someone else. Anxiety, stress and unfamiliar surroundings and people can all have an impact upon our memory.

Attention and concentration
Fatigue, environment, medication, time of day and physical health, including infections, can all have a big impact upon this. Be mindful of this throughout your assessment.

Reasoning
Individuals may feel very threatened with questions being 'thrown' at them and what might be considered 'unreasonable' or a sign of lack of capacity may actually be a perfectly reasonable reaction to your unreasonable style of assessment.

Information processing
How a person interprets what s/he is told is important to bear in mind. Some people may take a while to 'download' and process what has been said. People 'staring into space' might not be a sign of being vacant but could actually be them reflecting on what you have said.

Verbal comprehension and all forms of communication
Think about the words you use when asking questions and someone's preferred method of communication and vocabulary range. Asking

someone if they 'feel bilious' may get a different result than if you asked them whether they 'feel sick'.

Cultural influences
Ethnicity, religion, beliefs, values and gender can determine how someone might interact with you and value your assessment (or not!). Being mindful of this and adapting your communication style or asking someone else to be present or to assess instead may be necessary for the person's needs.

How do we record capacity?
This is an interesting question because it often feels like the wrong question to actually be asking. Many practitioners may instead ask, *'Do we have to record assessments of capacity?'*. The very simple answer to this question is yes and no because it all depends on how you determine a mental capacity assessment. For day-to-day assessments of capacity that involve routine levels of care and minimal interventions, such as making a decision on behalf of Mrs Sheikh that she has cornflakes for breakfast because she enjoys them but lacks the capacity to make that decision for herself, would not necessarily warrant a recording of an assessment of capacity as this would then turn basic care and decision-making into a complex bureaucratic process resulting in reams of unnecessary paperwork.

What needs to be considered here is that as the complexity of the decision increases, so should the need to record clearly the assessment of capacity and what the triggers were for the assessment.

Any assessment of capacity must follow the DAD process (decision, assessment and determination) as referred to above having gone through the two-stage test for capacity. Developing a mental capacity assessment form could be of use to you and your agency, but what must not be done is for these to be routinely filled in and placed in people's records as a mechanism to defend and protect practitioners so that they can say they have ticked certain boxes. Do remember that the person is always assumed to have capacity unless there is evidence to substantiate otherwise.

Earlier in this chapter we looked at less complex and complex decisions (which are also considered in Chapter 6). It would be appropriate for your record of assessment of capacity to reflect these two types of decision.

A recording form for assessing mental capacity should include:

1. Individual's details

>Name:

>Address:

>Date of birth:

>Location at time of assessment:

2. Decision requiring assessment of mental capacity (provide details)

3. Two-stage test of mental capacity

a. Does the person have an impairment of the mind or brain, or is there some sort of disturbance affecting the way their mind or brain works? (It doesn't matter whether the impairment or disturbance is temporary or permanent.) Provide evidence:

b. Does the impairment or disturbance mean that the person is unable to make the decision in question at the time it needs to be made?

c. Can the person:

>a. Understand information relevant to the decision? Yes/No

>b. Evidence:

>c. Retain that information? Yes/No

>d. Evidence:

>e. Use or weigh that information as part of the process of making a decision? Yes/No

>f. Evidence:

>g. Communicate his/her decision (whether by talking or by other means)? Yes/No

>h. Evidence:

If a person cannot do one or more of these, they are unable to make the decision.

4. Outcome of mental capacity assessment
On the balance of probabilities, there is a reasonable belief that:

The person *does/does not* (delete as applicable) have the mental capacity to make this specific decision at this time.

Name/details/signature of assessor and date.

Source: Kent & Medway MCA Local Implementation Network (2009).

Planned capacity assessments for more complex decisions that may include a best interests meeting being held in order to agree the specific decision should be asking more questions and considering more aspects than a less complex decision. For example, it is important to ensure that thorough consultation takes place as there is a duty to do this under the MCA. Consulting does not mean giving information to (therefore potentially breaching confidentiality) but seeking information from others in order to gather more information and form a holistic overview of P and his/her needs.

S.4(6) of the MCA states that the decision-maker *must take into account*, if it is practicable and appropriate to consult them, the views of:

- Anyone named by the person as someone to be consulted on the matter in question or on matters of that kind.
- Anyone engaged in caring for the person or interested in his/her welfare.
- Any IMCA.
- Any Lasting Power of Attorney (LPA) granted by the person.
- Any Deputy appointed for the person by the Court.

The person undertaking the assessment of capacity (who may or may not be the decision-maker) should also take into account the views of the above.

The above box tells us something that is worth noting and being aware of, in that family members and next of kin are not mentioned specifically. Of course, it may well be the case that a family member or next of kin falls into one of these categories and this should be considered fully and appropriately so that, with P's permission, or if it is deemed in P's best interests, they can be consulted and be present to support P during the capacity assessment, particularly if the decision is of significant importance to P. The person assessing capacity will need to be clear about their determination and whether the capacity assessment can in fact wait if it is not urgent or if P is likely to regain capacity.

The General Medical Council (GMC) offers guidance to doctors in relation to seeking consent for treatment and refers to the MCA. This guidance is helpful in reinforcing that acquiring consent and assessing capacity if need be are not separate entities. In fact, one can only consent to a course of treatment if one has the mental capacity to do so.

Consent guidance: Assessing capacity (GMC)

71. You must assess a patient's capacity to make a particular decision at the time it needs to be made. You must not assume that because a patient lacks capacity to make a decision on a particular occasion, they lack capacity to make any decisions at all, or will not be able to make similar decisions in the future.

72. You must take account of the advice on assessing capacity in the Codes of Practice that accompany the *Mental Capacity Act 2005 and the Adults with Incapacity (Scotland) Act 2000* and other relevant guidance. If your assessment is that the patient's capacity is borderline, you must be able to show that it is more likely than not that they lack capacity.

73. If your assessment leaves you in doubt about the patient's capacity to make a decision, you should seek advice from:

1. nursing staff or others involved in the patient's care, or those close to the patient, who may be aware of the patient's usual ability to make decisions and their particular communication needs

2. colleagues with relevant specialist experience, such as psychiatrists, neurologists, or speech and language therapists.

74. If you are still unsure about the patient's capacity to make a decision, you must seek legal advice with a view to asking a court to determine capacity.

From Consent: Patients and Doctors Making Decisions Together. GMC (2014).

What this guidance makes reference to is consultation and seeking advice from others and if need be consulting with the Court of

Protection who not only can make decisions in P's best interests, but can make determinations of capacity.

This chapter has sought to demystify the process of assessing capacity by looking at triggers for assessment and explaining that capacity is only assessed if a decision is to be made and there is doubt about P's ability to make that decision. The two-stage test for capacity has been considered, but most importantly what has been presented is that relationships, skills and value-laden practice are at the centre of engaging people in their own capacity assessment in order to ensure that P's wishes, feelings and preferences are, as far as is possible, at the centre of the decision-making process. Assessing capacity can be an informal process and an act which is done by staff with little awareness to it in relation to day-to-day decisions, but it can also be a major piece of work requiring consultation and deep reflection into the use of self.

It is suggested that the key skill is knowing the difference between the two, and ensuring that people's care is not overly bureaucratized and that vulnerable adults do not become pawns in risk averse practice. Reflecting always on why practitioners might assess someone's capacity and the ethical issues behind this will support the application in practice of the The Principles of the MCA. Of particular importance is principle number one – a person must be assumed to have mental capacity unless it is established that he lacks capacity. It is within that process of establishing a lack of capacity that we shine a light on values, agendas, risk and cultures of accountability. Place the person and their wishes, feelings and preferences at the centre of that practice and you won't go far wrong.

Chapter 4

Advocacy and Empowerment

What is advocacy?

There are several definitions of advocacy, but it is commonly accepted that advocacy is about supporting someone to have their views, wishes and voice heard and ensuring their rights are upheld and acted upon. A person who accesses advocacy is often in a position in their lives where others have power over them, which means they may feel or are unable to articulate or feel confident in expressing themselves. They may be unaware of their rights or services that they're entitled to. Advocacy ensures that the person at the heart of decision-making is able to participate fully in whatever the decision is, be it day-to-day events or long-term major life-changing decisions.

History of advocacy

In the UK we can see the history of advocacy as far back as the 1790s where James Tilly Matthews, a tobacco merchant, volunteered to act as a mediator during the war between France and Britain. He was imprisoned in 1793 until 1796, after which the French began to be suspicious of him, believing he was a spy. On his release he was sent back to England where he broke into the House of Lords and shouted at Lord Liverpool, '*Traitor!*'

Having previously been an aide to Lord Liverpool, he was angry at the lack of political intervention during his imprisonment. Resulting in immediate arrest, Tilly was transferred to Bethlam hospital (now known as the South London and Maudsley NHS Foundation Trust). Tilly later became the subject of Haslam's 1810 book, '*Illustrations of Madness*'. Haslam was the apothecary in charge of Bethlam hospital who began studying Tilly's psychotic visions and experiences. This is considered to be the first documented account of schizophrenia. Whilst detained in hospital Tilly wrote about the conditions of Bethlam, which resulted in his friends and family campaigning for his release, and subsequently meant the conditions were inspected and later used in redesigning the hospital. Tilly was later moved to a Quaker hospital, Foxes, in 1814 where he became the private secretary of Doctor Fox. This was an early form of advocacy demonstrated, by those who knew James Tilly Matthews, that supported his voice to be heard by those in a position of power and which led to improvement in the care and environment for patients at Bethlam.

Since this time we have seen advocacy become a core part of working with vulnerable people who may be or feel disempowered, experience stigma or discrimination due to their mental health, diagnosis, age, social standing or ethnicity to name a few. This was influenced by Wolf Wolfensberger who developed citizen advocacy in the 1980s (Wolfensberger and Zauha 1973). Citizen advocacy is a form of advocacy carried out largely by unpaid volunteers who spend time getting to know the person they are working with (usually someone with a learning disability) including what their wishes and views are, what preferences they have in a range of daily living activities, their preferred way of communicating, likes and dislikes etc. This enables the advocate to represent the person by ensuring others involved in the person's life know about them as much as they do and using what they know about the person to input into their daily care and relevant decisions.

In the 1980s, the majority of advocacy was carried out on behalf of someone who was unable to instruct the advocate; that is they may have been able to express a view or preference, but unable to instruct the advocate as to the specific actions they would like them to take. Advocacy was often taking place in long-term institutions where many clients were unable to give instruction to the advocate, either because they were unable to or because their opportunities were limited in terms of being able to develop communication skills.

As a result of the Mental Capacity Act receiving Royal Assent in April 2005, the first statutory advocacy service/role to support adults, was created, known as Independent Mental Capacity Advocate (IMCA). In 2005 seven IMCA pilot projects across the country were commissioned for 18 months to roll out this service to enable guidance for commissioners as well as addressing some of the key terms of the Act such as 'lack of capacity', 'appropriate to consult' and how to assess the quality of the service. The Act came into force October 2007, but the IMCA service was the first part of its implementation and commenced in England April 2007.

Instructed advocacy

Ben has obsessive compulsive disorder (OCD) and one of the ways this manifests itself is that he hoards numerous items including newspapers, magazines, cardboard and pieces of paper that he's been given throughout the day (receipts, bus tickets). This is now having an impact on his tenancy with the council who are threatening to evict him. Ben fully understands that his OCD is an illness and is receiving support from the local community mental health team (CMHT) including input from a therapist that specializes in working with people who have OCD. Ben would like support to write to the council and arrange a meeting to discuss his illness as believes if the council understand what the issue is they will allow him to continue with his tenancy until he is in more of a position to maintain his immediate environment. He contacts an advocate who specializes in working with people who have OCD, as they understand what his housing rights and options are. Ben is able to tell the advocate what role he would like her to have in meetings, what he is able to talk about without support and what he would like her to lead on. He understands she is independent of the local authority and CMHT and is employed by a charity that receives external funding to provide advocacy.

Non-instructed advocacy

Edna is an older person with a diagnosis of dementia, and currently detained under Section 2 of the Mental Health Act. An advocate from the local advocacy provider for this hospital approaches Edna on the ward as he notices she is a new patient and he wishes to explain who he is. Edna initially appears to understand what the advocate does and she informs him that she knows where she is and recognizes she has been experiencing memory problems which she believes the staff team are concerned about. She explains that she wishes to return home as soon as the staff have carried out what they need to do. The advocate visits Edna the next day, but she has no memory of meeting the previous day. She appears quite disorientated and distressed, and the staff team tell the advocate that this is a bad day for Edna; her presentation is similar to that on her admission. The advocate therefore needs to carry out non-instructed advocacy as Edna's ability to fully instruct the advocate is impaired at this time.

Like all decisions that need to be made under the Mental Capacity Act, instructing an advocate (not an IMCA whereby their instruction is based on whether the person has the capacity to make a specific decision – detailed further in the chapter) is still decision-specific and the person needs to:

- understand what the advocate does

- retain that information

- use and weigh up information related to this

- communicate that they would like to advocate representing them.

This may fluctuate and it is important to continue to re-visit the person's capacity on this decision.

Interestingly, we have seen a move away from non-instructed advocacy and a report *Advocating for Equality* (2001) by the Independent Advocacy Campaign[1] established that advocacy providers were far less likely to provide advocacy for people with communication and profound multiple impairments than any other group of people. It also established that the majority of services were commissioned to provide instructed advocacy. Whilst advocacy is about supporting disempowered people to be empowered in decisions in their lives and ensure their voice is listened to, those unable to instruct an advocate can be left without this support. This means that some of the most vulnerable people in society are left unable to access advocacy.

This is an issue that was importantly addressed by the Mental Capacity Act. Whilst there is still a long way to go in terms of training and understanding of how to deliver non-instructed advocacy and what it should look like, not just for advocates, but for professionals involved with this client group, the role of the IMCA is supporting that development.

Models of non-instructed advocacy

It is important at this stage just to focus on the five key models that make up non-instructed advocacy to understand the background to the role of an IMCA, as well as ensuring that there is an understanding as to how a non-instructed advocate would work with a client when that person may not be eligible for an IMCA.

---

1   See www.aqvx59.dsl.pipex.com/Advocating%20for%20Equality.pdf for more information.

Historically there have been four models associated with non-instructed advocacy but in recent years a fifth model was added as a way of capturing any further issues or questions that the advocate wanted to ask of the relevant decision-makers.

- **Rights-based model:** Focusing on the person's basic fundamental human rights. The advocate's role is to ensure that the person's basic human rights are promoted, upheld and actioned upon including where the advocate believes the person's rights are being violated or abused, then they would seek to address this, which may include seeking legal advice and/or representation for the person.

- **Witness observer model:** This is where the advocate might spend time with the person observing how they interact with others/the environment around them by way of getting to know them. This approach does not expect the advocate to make judgments, but rather report on their observations or raise issues with others that they may had been previously unaware of or had been overlooked, for example, a lack of or over-stimulation, reactions to noises or other people.

- **Watching brief:** A model that originated within the Citizens Advice Bureau and later developed into what we know it as now, by ASIST. It focuses on eight domains of quality of life including individuality; wellbeing; community presence and relationships (amongst others) and uses a series of questions to enable representation.

- **Person-centred model:** This focuses on getting to know the person and what is important in their life and out of all the models requires more time in order to get to know the person, their likes, dislikes, preferences and what is important to the person. This in turn then promotes a person-centred approach within decision-making by promoting the uniqueness of the person.

- **Questioning approach:** Probably the most informal of all the models, but it has the aim of giving 'permission' to the advocate to ask questions either of decision-makers or about the decision at hand that may not have been captured yet.

The aim of non-instructed advocacy is to try to combine all models, using the advocate's own judgement as well as using the models to fit within the time frame that's available. For example, if an advocate meets with a client only hours before a decision-making meeting, it may be more appropriate to use the rights-based and questioning model, given that there will have been limited time to spend with the person and get to know them in any depth.

The MCA brought in a framework known as the best interests checklist, a series of factors that need to be considered before making a decision on a person's behalf. This checklist is required to be used by all professionals when working within the framework of the Act, and has solidified the role of the IMCA with regards to non-instructed advocacy by serving as a further model for them in carrying out their role.

Principle of independence

One of the most important principles of advocacy is that advocates are independent from other service providers of health and social care, for example, the Local Authority or NHS. This is to ensure there is no conflict of interest with regards to their ability to fully represent the person. For example, social workers, nurses, doctors, care home managers, providers of domiciliary or other support services all have a very specific remit with regards to the person. They are responsible for making certain decisions about the person – decisions that the person may or may not agree with; they have a specific duty of care and accountability, which differs from that of an advocate. That is not to say that they can't or don't use advocacy skills, but rather that they have dual responsibilities, whereas an advocate's role is very specific to representing the person in a variety of ways. Below are some examples about the importance of independent advocacy:

Case studies
(Please note that instructed advocacy within the Mental Health Act has been included in the second case study to demonstrate the meaning of independence.)

Jessica is a 65-year-old woman with dementia and has been deemed to lack capacity to make a decision about where she should live. She is currently in respite following a fall at home. She is able to tell the advocate that she wants to return home. The advocate progresses this and raises questions as well as presenting options available to the decision-maker. The decision-maker presents the options to the funding panel (which is the Local Authority who the decision-maker works for). Both options (returning home with a package of care or moving into a care home) would meet Jessica's needs, but there are vast differences in costs. The panel decide that the most affordable package of care that would meet Jessica's needs, is a care home. At this stage the decision-maker cannot progress anything further on behalf of Jessica as only elements of this decision are for her to decide. The advocate, however, can challenge this on behalf of Jessica; they can seek legal advice and representation for Jessica.

Jimmy has a diagnosis of schizophrenia and is currently detained under the Mental Health Act. He approaches his advocate to request support in obtaining leave to return to his home town for a visit. The advocate initially approaches the care team without Jimmy – at his request – and is informed that the team has made a decision that he will not be allowed leave for the time being, therefore there is no point in this being raised in the forthcoming ward round. The advocate explains his role is to channel issues on behalf of Jimmy and not filter them and asks that they explain this fact to Jimmy, as he has not been made aware that this is the case.

The team informs the advocate that they do not believe leave is in his best interests and so repeat that they will not discuss it in ward rounds. When the advocate meets with Jimmy again he asks for an update on his leave and the advocate explains the team have made a decision he cannot have leave. Jimmy still wishes for the advocate to progress this issue and so he approaches the team again and explains that an element of his role is about representing the issues the person wishes and that even if the decision is not in line with what Jimmy wants he has a right to have his voice heard. The team therefore agree to discuss further with Jimmy, and his psychiatrist explains their rationale. From this Jimmy has improved understanding about the decision-making and whilst it does not stop his desire for leave, the advocacy role has facilitated Jimmy's involvement in his own care, increased awareness, understanding and communication. If the advocate had worked for the mental health team and been in a position of deciding what's best for Jimmy as oppose to being his representative this could not have occurred.

Retaining this independence can present issues for advocacy providers, including IMCAs. One of the reasons for this is that many advocacy providers receive funding from the local authority to provide advocacy. Where there is a legal duty to provide advocacy in England and Wales, the government arrangements are that they will fund this, but provide local authority commissioners with the funding. It is then for commissioners to invite organizations to tender for contracts. There are engagement protocols and service level agreements in place that ensure the advocacy service retains its independence with regards to recruitment, management, supervision and overall employee responsibilities. The local authority cannot influence any of these factors and it is a transparent process.

The advocacy provider also retains confidentiality and would not disclose personal or identifiable details of those that access the service. Contract monitoring meetings take place between commissioners of a local authority and the advocacy provider which can look at a range of issues such as the number of people accessing the service, demographic monitoring, whether the advocacy provider has identified areas of concern within their advocacy practice (for example, if they provided advocacy in one particular unit and clients were consistently raising the same concern that was not being addressed) and so on.

Similarly, the advocacy provider has similar systems in place to ensure it does not have a conflict with itself as an organization. For example, a mental health charity may provide a range of services such as housing schemes or employment support services and not just advocacy. In areas where they have been commissioned to provide advocacy, agreements are made within the organization itself as well as with the local authority that they will not provide other services aside from advocacy in that locality. This ensures that there is transparency and reduces any conflict of interest, that is, the advocate will not be put in a position of effectively challenging decisions made by their own organization such as a housing scheme, or indeed in a position of promoting a service that their employer provides.

Case study

John is unhappy with the support he's receiving in the supported living accommodation he resides in and approaches an advocate for support in addressing his areas of concern. The advocacy service provides supported living for people with mental health needs, but not in this local area. Due to the service level agreement in place, the supported accommodation is provided by another housing provider, which enables the advocate to represent John without any conflict. This also means that should John wish to move, the organization that provides the advocacy service does not have any housing schemes in that locality, leaving the advocate free of any potential conflict should John wish to move.

However, the fact that local authorities provide the funding for advocacy providers to carry out their role can still present some problems. For example, some people who access the advocacy service, when they become aware of this, may be of the view that this means the advocacy service is effectively working on behalf of the local authority. Although this is not the case, the person (who may wish for the advocacy service to support them in challenging a decision made by the local authority) can sometimes feel hampered or suspicious in accessing the service.

Similarly and in particular regard to an IMCA service, this may present a problem when they are challenging a decision made by the local authority (for example, where a person should live) *or* when they wish to progress this challenge to the Court of Protection. Court proceedings can be hugely costly to local authorities and some providers can feel that they are effectively taking their own commissioners to court and that this may impact on their ability to retain their contract. Some IMCA providers have shared anonymous stories of commissioners, implying the loss of a contract if they progress an issue to court (Cowley 2014). Whilst an IMCA is merely carrying out their role if they do this and it is clear within the Act itself that they have this right and it is not overstepping the boundaries or agreements in place, it can still feel quite daunting. There is an argument because of this that commissioning should be centrally controlled by an independent organization, but there are problems with this idea. Some advocacy providers feel that local commissioning is the better option because it means decisions about contracts and tenders are based on local knowledge and experience. There is also a view that there is a risk in losing local advocacy provision that is provided by a relatively small organization in comparison to larger advocacy providers who may be better resourced in terms of competing for tenders. There is a case for both sides of the argument and it is not an issue that can be answered within this book, but it is worth highlighting to understand some of the issues the advocacy sector is faced with.

Role of the Independent Mental Capacity Advocate (IMCA)

The Code of Practice describes the IMCA service's aims as:

To help particularly vulnerable people who lack the capacity to make important decisions about serious medical treatment and changes of accommodation, and who have no family or friends that it would be appropriate to consult about those decisions. IMCAs will work with and support people who lack capacity, and represent their views to those who are working out their best interests.

The service is commissioned by the Local Authority that receives funding from the Department of Health on an annual basis as part of the responsibility to ensure its delivery as a statutory advocacy role and is available Monday to Friday between office hours. The service is not expected to be available as an emergency response, but where a decision about a person has been taken in an emergency, for example, medical treatment at Accident & Emergency, or as a result of an immediate care home closure, an IMCA should be instructed as soon as possible after the decision and where it remains appropriate, namely, where it fits the criteria.

The Code of Practice describes the role of an IMCA as to:

- Confirm that the person instructing them has the authority to do so.

- Interview or meet in private the person who lacks capacity, if possible.

- Act in accordance with the principles of the Act and take account of relevant guidance in the Code of Practice.

- Examine any relevant records that section 35(6) of the Act gives them access to.

- Get the views of professionals and paid workers providing care or treatment for the person who lacks capacity.

- Obtain the views of anybody else who can give information about the wishes and feelings, beliefs or values of the person who lacks capacity.

- Get hold of any other information they think will be necessary.

- Find out what support a person who lacks capacity has had to help them make the specific decision.

- Try to find out what the person's wishes and feelings, beliefs and values would be likely to be if the person had capacity.

- Find out what alternative options there are.

- Consider whether getting another medical opinion would help the person who lacks capacity.

- Write a report on their findings for the local authority or NHS body.

IMCAs within their role may also:

- Raise or ask relevant questions related to the person and/or decision.

- Highlight alternative options in regards to the decision.

- Use the relevant complaints procedures where there is a disagreement either about the process or the decision itself.

- Challenge the decision and apply to the Court of Protection (for further information refer to the section on the role of Litigation Friend).

Responsibility to instruct an IMCA

The Mental Capacity Act states that IMCAs must be instructed by the 'responsible body', that is, the Local Authority or NHS (essentially the body responsible overall for making the decision) and by an authorized person. Regulations (The Mental Capacity Act 2005 (Independent Mental Capacity Advocates) (General) Regulations 2006) define an authorized person as a person who is *'required or enabled to instruct an IMCA'*. An authorized person could be a consultant, a nurse or social worker. Responsible bodies can also authorize other bodies or organizations to instruct an IMCA.

In practice, whilst the decision-maker (person within the responsible body named as having a duty to make the decision at hand) does not have to be the person that instructs the IMCA, they and their employer do have to make sure that there is a process in place to ensure instruction occurs as soon as possible.

Criteria of instruction

Where there is a reasonable belief that the person lacks capacity to make the decision and there are no family or friends 'appropriate to consult' an IMCA *must* be instructed in the following circumstances:

- An NHS body or local authority is proposing to arrange accommodation (or a change of accommodation) in hospital (where the person will *stay in hospital longer than 28 days*) or a care home (*for more than eight weeks*).

- An NHS body is proposing to provide serious medical treatment.

There are also two discretionary decisions where an IMCA *may* be instructed by the Local Authority or NHS, where it is felt the person will benefit from an IMCA in matters concerning:

- care reviews, and

- adult safeguarding cases, *whether or not family, friends or others are involved.*

Accommodation decisions and IMCA involvement

The majority of decisions that require IMCA involvement are decisions about where a person should live and the following are examples of where an IMCA instruction may occur:

Case studies

Sandra has a diagnosis of dementia and has had a fall at home. She is admitted to hospital and during her treatment and admission it becomes apparent that she lacks the capacity to make certain decisions including where she should live on discharge. A proposal for her to go into respite for six weeks is made, but as a safeguard an IMCA is instructed in case the respite goes on longer than six weeks or a decision is made that long-term accommodation is in her best interests.

Joey suffered a stroke and was admitted to hospital from home; he is recovering well and a stay on a rehab ward is proposed for the next few weeks before further decisions about care and treatment are made. As he is likely to be in hospital for more than 28 days and is unable to consent to this, an IMCA is instructed.

Lou has a diagnosis of schizophrenia and dementia. She lives at home on her own and is under the care of the older persons' care team within the local authority. They have supported her to remain at home for some time, but now believe the risks of this are too high and are proposing she move into longer-term accommodation; an IMCA is instructed.

Jenny has a learning disability and lives in supported accommodation. This was initially meant to be a temporary home until more appropriate accommodation could be sought that catered more specifically for Jenny's needs. Whilst she has settled in very well during the last six months, a proposal is made that she move into the new home. An IMCA is instructed as part of the best interests decision-making process.

As in all decisions, the role of the IMCA is to meet with the person, ascertain their wishes, highlight options where applicable, and gather the views of others in order to input into the best interests process.

Case study

Sean is an ex drug user and as a result of several seizures he had when using, he has an acquired brain injury. Following a prolonged epileptic fit at home he is admitted to hospital. His communication is impaired and it is determined that he lacks capacity to make a decision about discharge. He has an ex-partner and young daughter whom he sees often, but they are deemed inappropriate as they request to be taken out of the decision-making process. An IMCA is instructed.

Sean's admission is lengthy so the IMCA has several weeks to get to know him, as well as his ex-partner, in order to gather further information about what is important to Sean. The IMCA also gathers information about Sean's usual daily routine, accesses his medical and social care records and speaks with all those who know Sean both in a personal and professional capacity.

Whilst Sean is now physically quite disabled and requires support in carrying out daily living activities, it is clear he is a very independent man with strong ties to his local community. From a clinical perspective there is little rehab that can be offered due to the long-term damage Sean has already experienced and the views of those involved are mixed, ranging from a suggestion of a long-term brain injury unit, to returning home. The consultant in charge believes that based on the evidence of Sean's history, a significant level of sedation would be required to enable a move into a long term unit which ethically he feels is not appropriate when a less restrictive option can be considered.

The decision-maker, Sean's social worker, believes that the provision of a care package at home would not be sufficient and believes a long-term unit would be more suitable; she believes that Sean would quickly settle in. The alternative would likely mean that Sean would need to be deprived of his liberty and that he would actively be against this. After gathering a wealth of evidence, the IMCA advocates that Sean return home with a package of care, which can include assisted technology to reduce risks. Sean's ex-partner, whilst deemed inappropriate is also advocating for this to ensure a continued relationship with their daughter and nearby friends. The IMCA also states that she would seek to request the decision is progressed to the Court of Protection should the decision-maker disagree with this option. This is because the weight of evidence supporting Sean's return home appears to outweigh the likely risks and detrimental impact on Sean based on the evidence presented.

Serious medical treatment and IMCA involvement

Serious medical treatment is defined as treatment which involves *giving new treatment, stopping treatment that has already started or withholding treatment* that could be offered in circumstances where:

- if a single treatment is proposed there is a fine balance between the likely benefits and the burdens to the patient and the risks involved

- a decision between a choice of treatments is finely balanced, or

- what is proposed is likely to have serious consequences for the patient.

'Serious consequences' are those which *could have a serious impact on the patient*, either from the effects of the treatment itself or its wider implications. This may include treatments which:

- cause serious and prolonged pain, distress or side effects

- have potentially major consequences for the patient (for example, stopping life-sustaining treatment or having major surgery such as heart surgery), or

- have a serious impact on the patient's future life choices (for example, interventions for ovarian cancer).

The simplest way to view serious medical treatment is to consider the impact of 'giving, stopping or withholding' treatment for the person. For example, a blood test may seem a relatively straightforward decision and procedure and therefore not viewed as serious medical treatment (albeit still a best interests decision where the person is unable to consent). However, the impact of a blood test may be extremely distressing for someone who cannot understand why it is being suggested. There may be a fine balance between the likely benefits and burdens, for example, it may highlight a medical issue but not be the only diagnostic test; or the burden faced by the person (they may have to be restrained which could impact on relationships with staff who know them well) outweighs its use. Like all decisions under the MCA, the person must remain at the heart of the process.

The Code of Practice outlines the following as serious medical treatment decisions that an IMCA could get involved in. This list is not exhaustive:

- chemotherapy and surgery for cancer

- electro-convulsive therapy

- therapeutic sterilization

- major surgery (such as open-heart surgery or brain/ neurosurgery)

- major amputations (for example, loss of an arm or leg)

- treatments which will result in permanent loss of hearing or sight

- withholding or stopping artificial nutrition and hydration

- termination of pregnancy.

The Department of Health annual report, *The Sixth Year of the Independent Mental Capacity Advocacy Service (IMCA): 2012/2013*, published in February 2014 details the range of treatment decisions IMCAs in England were instructed for:

Decision	Number of IMCA instructions 2012/2013
Other	597
Medical investigations	338
Do Not Attempt Cardiopulmonary Resuscitation	264
Serious dental work	223
Cancer treatment	127
Major surgery	69

cont.

Decision	Number of IMCA instructions 2012/2013
Not specified	65
Clinically assisted nutrition and hydration	60
Affecting hearing/sight	46
Hip/leg operations	27
Major amputations	18
Electroconvulsive therapy (ECT)	12
Pregnancy termination	3
Not known	56
Total	**1907**

Case study: Serious medical treatment

Sarah is in a care home where she has lived for the last seven years; prior to this she was in a psychiatric hospital and had been there for over 40 years. Staff at the home have noticed she has been losing weight quite rapidly recently and take her to see the GP. The GP refers Sarah to see a gastroenterologist at the local hospital for further investigations. Initially staff escort her to an outpatient appointment, but on seeing the hospital, Sarah becomes extremely distressed and hits one of the care staff (they think this has triggered memories of her previous stay in hospital and that she believes she's returning to a psychiatric unit).

On the 2nd appointment, Sarah runs away from staff when they arrive at the hospital. At this point the gastroenterologist requests that Sarah's psychiatrist carries out a capacity assessment to determine whether she has the capacity to understand the decision to have a CT scan (the proposed initial investigative procedure). He concludes she does not have capacity and instructs the IMCA service.

The IMCA goes to meet with Sarah and spends some time at the home; Sarah does not particularly engage with her and continually wanders away. Staff describe this as quite typical for Sarah, stating she's constantly on the move and this is something they need to keep an eye on, as due to her gait she often trips and falls. Sarah has a diagnosis of schizophrenia and is often observed responding to voices; this appears to be her main form of communication and the impact of such a long-term stay in hospital is evident with regards to her behaviour.

The IMCA spends time speaking to staff and investigating through questions and reading through Sarah's notes to gain further insight into Sarah's personality as well as the history behind this current decision. The IMCA visits on four more occasions over a period of ten days, spending time observing Sarah, trying to engage with staff and speaking with them about their relationship with Sarah as well as her relationship with other residents. The IMCA speaks with Sarah's psychiatrist to understand her mental health history, her GP to gather some further medical history and the gastroenterologist in order to gather the full facts about the procedure before submitting her report.

The IMCA summarizes the above in order to convey to the decision-maker (gastroenterologist) a full picture of Sarah that includes key information about how she responds to hospital environments as well as an update with regards to her weight and the initial concerns that staff raised.

The IMCA concludes that it would appear not to be in Sarah's best interests for the procedure to go ahead. She notes the following to substantiate this:

- Sarah has gained the weight she initially lost.

- She is physically active for most of the day and her diet (food intake) varies dependent on her mood.

- The impact of her psychiatric long-term admission is very marked and the level of distress she experiences on merely approaching a hospital suggests she is unlikely to physically make it through the door.

- When Sarah has a yearly flu injection, the GP and nurse have to visit her at the home; after a period of years she has become used to this, but there is detailed planning in the carrying out of this activity in order to ensure that Sarah is reassured, relaxed and able to consent.

- Sarah is not demonstrating any difference in her behaviour, she does not appear (according to staff observations) in any physical pain.

- To end, the need for Sarah to have further investigations appears to be driven by the care home staff as opposed to Sarah exhibiting any physical health concerns or symptoms. This is not a criticism as it is evident they care and wish the best for Sarah, but there is a risk that more weight has been placed on this factor rather than Sarah's preferences.

- The IMCA asks that all this be taken into account before the gastroenterologist decides whether there is still a need for any investigations. She also states that if he concludes this is clinically necessary (as it is this factor that appears finely balanced) then time will need to be spent with Sarah and the home in trying to address whether any desensitization can take place; whether sedation would need to be considered and lastly whether any actions may result in a deprivation of liberty. Continued IMCA involvement would be necessary should the decision be for the CT scan to go ahead and may involve a request by the IMCA for this decision to go to the Court of Protection depending on the outcome of the varying issues.

The above is based on a real case and is an example of the range of actions IMCAs will carry out and how they will best represent the person. There will be further information about the writing of reports later in this chapter.

Compliance with the Mental Capacity Act in hospital

Historically it has remained an ongoing concern that there is a lack of instructions to IMCA providers for serious medical treatment decisions. Most notable is the fact that the majority of IMCA instructions are for long-term accommodation *and* the person is in hospital at the time of instruction. Whilst the number of accommodation decisions were expected (according to the Department of Health impact assessment) to be high and the figures for them are in line with predictions, the fact the person is already in hospital suggests something is awry.

The number of serious medical treatment decisions to date has remained well below (over two-thirds) the estimated figure (even seven years, at the time of writing, on since the implementation of the Act). Although capacity is decision-specific, it is reasonable to hypothesize that there cannot be a high number of people that are able to consent (and therefore have capacity) to medical treatment yet unable to make a decision about where to live on their discharge. Many IMCAs also anecdotally talk of the fact that there is evidence within the person's medical notes that many of these treatment decisions were in fact best interests decisions, be it recorded as such or simply carried out without any formal process. Where they have been noted as actual best interests decisions, a referral to the IMCA was not made. It is also important to highlight that where a person is likely to remain in hospital for more than 28 days either as part of a planned or unplanned admission, there also remains the duty to instruct an IMCA, yet IMCA services across the country report this does not happen.

There is no other detailed formal recording of MCA compliance other than that of the IMCA service and whilst it is a small part of the Act, the figures and information generated by the Department of Health annual IMCA reports is still a significant insight into compliance amongst other professions and localities.

The reasons for this appear vast and at times complex, but information gathering carried out by the two national IMCA projects that sat within SCIE and Action for Advocacy considered the following issues:

- NHS professionals by and large do not work within a system where they make external referrals.

- Internal systems such as NHS intranets may not support the option of having external organizations' information.

- Advocacy remains by and large a role that exists in social care and therefore is still a relatively new service within the health service.

- Decisions are sometimes viewed as purely clinical decisions rather than best interests decisions.

- A person's non-refusal of medical treatment can be interpreted as consent and therefore capacity queried only at the point where a person objects.

- IMCA services are not sufficiently resourced to enable them to carry out awareness and information sessions.

- In some NHS Trusts the MCA is not a mandatory part of the training programme, which can impact on it being embedded within practice.

- Assessments of capacity may not be carried out until a person is medically fit for discharge. This can then be viewed as local authority responsibility which means the instruction may be delayed until someone is appointed from the local authority to make the best interests decision (although an instruction can still be made by the hospital in preparation for this to enable timely IMCA involvement).

- Decisions may not be viewed as serious because they're relatively routine procedures. Referral to the actual criteria for what is considered serious medical treatment within the Act must occur in these situations.

(Empowerment Matters 2012)

It is vital that these issues are addressed where applicable, to ensure that the person who lacks capacity to make a decision either about remaining in hospital, being admitted to hospital for a period of time or serious medical treatment is afforded their legal right to an advocate and to be represented within best interests decisions.

Care Reviews and IMCA instruction

The Code of Practice details the criteria for involvement of an IMCA in Care Reviews.

A responsible body can instruct an IMCA to support and represent a person who lacks capacity when:

- they have arranged accommodation for that person

- they aim to review the arrangements (as part of a care plan or otherwise), and

- there are no family or friends who it would be appropriate to consult

- the decision-maker must be satisfied that having an IMCA will be of particular benefit to the person who lacks capacity.

Section 7 of the Local Authority Social Services Act 1970 sets out current requirements for care reviews. It states that there should be a review 'within three months of help being provided or major changes made to services.' There should then be a review every year – or more often, if needed.

Reviews should relate to decisions about accommodation:

- for someone who lacks capacity to make a decision about accommodation

- that will be provided for a continuous period of more than 12 weeks

- that are not the result of an obligation under the Mental Health Act 1983, and

- that do not relate to circumstances where sections 37 to 39 of the Act would apply.

Where the person is to be detained or required to live in accommodation under the Mental Health Act 1983 (amended 2007), an IMCA will not be needed since the safeguards available under that Act will apply.

Guidance for IMCAs in Care Reviews (SCIE Guide 39, 2013) recommends that the IMCA should:

- Read the current community care assessment, care plan and nursing needs assessments and check whether they include the person's preferences.

- Access any assessment and care plans produced by the service in relation to the individual.

- Focus not just on the choice of the accommodation, but also the support which will be received in that accommodation.

- Check that the support will be personalized.

- Try to get local authority care plans to clearly identify how specific needs will be met in the care plan. This should include who will provide the support, how often and for how long (e.g. supported to walk to the paper shop seven days a week).

- Establish whether the new service has good information about the person's history, interests and wishes. If not, consider providing a summary.

- Explore how you and others can enable the client to be as involved as much as possible in the decision-making process.

(SCIE 2013)

Many IMCAs will have been involved in the decision that precedes the care review instruction, for example, where there's been a change of accommodation or treatment. Their role will then be looking at the process that has occurred since this change and how the person themselves feels or has responded. There are, however, a number of non-statutory advocacy organizations that may be instructed for annual reviews, or the person may have an advocate already involved, meaning the need to instruct an IMCA is unnecessary.

Safeguarding and IMCA instruction

The Code of Practice details the criteria for involvement of an IMCA in Adult Safeguarding.

Responsible bodies have powers to instruct an IMCA to support and represent a person who lacks capacity where it is alleged that:

- the person is or has been abused or neglected by another person, or

- the person is abusing or has abused another person.

The responsible bodies can only instruct an IMCA if they propose to take, or have already taken, protective measures. This is in accordance with adult protection procedures set up under statutory guidance.

In adult protection cases (and no other cases), access to IMCAs is not restricted to people who have no-one else to support or represent them. People who lack capacity who have family and friends can still have an IMCA to support them in the adult protection procedures.

In some situations, a case may start out as an adult protection case where a local authority may consider whether or not to involve an IMCA under the criteria they have set – but may then become a case where the allegations or evidence give rise to the question of whether the person should be moved in their best interests. In these situations the case has become one where an IMCA must be involved if there is no-one else appropriate to support and represent the person in this decision.

In practice and in line with the regulations, this means that IMCAs *may* be instructed when there is a:

- proposal to take or have taken, protective measures in relation to a person who

- lacks capacity to agree to one or more of the measures

- where safeguarding adults proceedings have been instigated

- the decision-maker must be satisfied that having an IMCA will be of particular benefit to the person who lacks capacity.

It is the above four points that provide clarity as to when an IMCA can be instructed and make clear that safeguarding proceedings must have commenced, as well as there being a reasonable belief that the person lacks capacity with regards to the protective measure.

Guidance for IMCAs in *'Practice guidance on the involvement of Independent Mental Capacity Advocates (IMCAs) in safeguarding adults'* (SCIE Guide 32, 2013) outlines the following as to when an IMCA should be instructed, with regards to the 'particular benefit' to the person.

1. Where there is a serious exposure to risk: risk of death; risk of serious physical injury or illness; risk of serious deterioration in physical or mental health; risk of serious emotional distress.

2. Where a life-changing decision is involved and consulting family or friends is compromised by the reasonable belief that they would not have the person's best interests at heart.

3. Where there is a conflict of views between the decision-makers regarding the best interests of the person.

4. Where there is a risk of financial abuse, which could have a serious impact on the person at risk's welfare. For example, where the loss of money would mean that they would be unable to afford to live in their current accommodation, or to pay for valued opportunities.

Case study

Simon is 23 years old and has a learning disability; he is admitted to hospital via ambulance after collapsing at home. He was, as a child, under the care of a consultant paediatrician who is asked to see Simon due to concerns raised by the treating consultant. Simon is very small in size and the consultant wants to know from the paediatrician if this is his normal presentation, i.e. related to his disability. The paediatrician visits Simon and instigates safeguarding procedures, stating that his presentation is similar to that of those held in concentration camps. He believes he has been neglected at home and has concerns about discharging him once he's well.

A referral is made to the IMCA service where an initial strategy meeting is held to discuss the protective measures, which are for Simon to be discharged to respite rather than home. Simon's mum is invited to the meeting, but does not attend, therefore the learning disability team visit her on two occasions over the next week and leave a note asking her to contact; she has yet to visit Simon on the ward. The IMCA meets with Simon on three occasions and although he doesn't verbally communicate and appears frightened when he first meets her he responds well when accompanied by the learning disability nurse whom he knows.

Two further meetings are held on the ward whilst Simon recuperates to discuss possible respite and the benefits of this for Simon. The learning disability team also catalogue their concerns over the last six months, but explain they have no evidence as such to back up their concerns that Simon is being physically neglected as Simon's mum does not respond to any phone calls, letters and has so far yet to attend a meeting. At the final meeting she attends and the concerns are put to her, but she states she is a good mum and wants Simon back home. She is unable to answer any questions about Simon's diet, why she has missed healthcare appointments that have been arranged for him and describes the use of a child buggy to mobilize Simon as 'easier all round'.

Due to the protective measure proposed, the IMCA suggests that what is being proposed (in light of mum's objections) is a Deprivation of Liberty. It is therefore felt appropriate to progress the issue to the Court of Protection as an urgent matter due to the fact Simon is almost ready for discharge.

The Care Act 2014 and advocacy instruction

The Care Act 2014, which comes into force in 2015, will bring in new responsibilities for Local Authorities to instruct an advocate where the person has substantial difficulty in being involved in the process of assessments (needs assessments or carers assessments); the review of care and support, or support arrangements, safeguarding enquiries or reviews.

Substantial difficulty means being unable to do one or more of the following (and where it has yet to be deemed that the person lacks capacity):

- understand relevant information

- retain that information

- use or weigh that information as part of the process of being involved

- communicate the individual's views, wishes and feelings (whether by talking, using sign language or any other means).

There is a clear crossover between the power to instruct an IMCA for care reviews/safeguarding and the duty to instruct an advocate under the Care Act for certain decisions. Whilst commissioning arrangements at the time of writing have yet to be published, requirements with regards an advocate's knowledge and skill base suggest that those qualified to work as IMCAs also carry out advocacy under the Care Act to ensure a streamlined crossover where people may lack capacity to make decisions. It is therefore highly possible that Care Act advocates and their involvement much earlier on in the process of care reviews and safeguarding will reduce the instruction of IMCAs in these decisions.

Deprivation of Liberty and IMCA instruction

The Deprivation of Liberty Safeguards (DoLS) introduced three additional IMCA roles – these are covered in more detail in Chapter 7.

'Appropriate to consult' and IMCA instruction

There has been much debate about what 'appropriate to consult' actually means and the Code of Practice does not offer a definition for this, but rather states that it is for the decision-maker to determine, in particular whether it is possible and practical to consult with others. For example, a family member may refuse to be consulted with, the person may have little contact with their family or family live in another part of the world where it is not practical to speak with them. Alternatively a family member or friend may have their own needs and issues going on and feel unable to be part of the process.

The Making Decisions Alliance (a former campaign group that supported the implementation of the Act) amongst others did not support the idea that people should be 'unbefriended' to be able to access independent advocacy. Indeed it can be argued that those who are befriended are actually at a disadvantage within the decision-making process. Family and/or friends may never have heard of the Act or had an opportunity to understand it until they find themselves in a situation where it applies. An IMCA can bring a wealth of knowledge not only about the Act but also relevant case law that others may not have. Family and friends are invested emotionally with the decision, which can make the process incredibly difficult, as whilst they are not responsible for making the decision, it is inevitable that they will feel some pressure to 'do the right thing'. And crucially there is no-one independent involved with the decision whose role it is to solely represent the person.

However, the criteria are clear that the IMCA service is only available for those who have no-one else (other than paid professionals) that are appropriate to consult or the decision-maker has deemed them not appropriate.

Referral/instruction process

There is no requirement for there to be written instruction and *IMCA Instruction: Best Practice Guidance* (Cowley and Lee 2010a) offers further guidance on this. However, for ease and speed of response, IMCA services have developed an instruction form that should be easily accessible from the relevant provider. Referral/ instructions can also take place over the phone.

There has been some criticism from external agencies that instructions forms are too lengthy when the decision-maker ultimately just wants the IMCA to respond. One of the main reasons for instruction forms appearing as they do is that services have a responsibility to input all information they receive from referrals (anonymized) on to a Department of Health database; this is still the only formal recording process and overview as to how the Act is working in different parts of the country. It is therefore beneficial for services to receive all of this in one go, but aside from that, it enables the IMCA service to prioritize referrals as well as gather what can be crucial information before they even meet the person. For example, what the person's communication needs are, or if there are family involved, the reason for them being deemed 'inappropriate' provides important information. Similarly the outcome of a capacity assessment and what the areas are that the person has difficulty with can enable an IMCA or the provider to allocate the case to someone who has particular skills in one area of communication. Equally this information can assist the IMCA to plan ahead as to the first meeting, for example, to take a picture board or gather information from a speech and language therapist that is involved with the person.

It might also be that there are IMCAs within a service that are more experienced in working with a particular client group (dementia, mental health, learning disabilities, brain injury and so on) which may benefit the person. Similarly, with regards to the decision, whilst IMCAs are not expected to be experts in all areas – ultimately they are there as the person's advocate, to gather the person's views and wishes, to understand the various elements of the decision and to ask questions on their behalf and then represent all of this within a meeting and report – it may be that they have gathered particular knowledge of PEG feeds or rehab processes after a stroke where this may benefit the person.

It's also important to consider that for most IMCA services, in reality there is only the equivalent of two or three full-time members of staff to cover a Local Authority or County; therefore anything that can streamline their work and ability to respond quickly and be informed must be a benefit for the person.

IMCA services should have in place prioritization policies that outline the response times once an instruction has been received. This would usually stipulate that there is a more rapid response for treatment decisions than, say, accommodation (although this is person- and decision-specific). For example, a person may be admitted to hospital on a Friday and the treatment decision for a PEG needs to be made by the following Wednesday; this is not usually the case for accommodation decisions. The 'power to instruct' decisions (safeguarding and care reviews) again will have to be responded to in a timeframe that considers the number of treatment and accommodation decisions, because the former are not statutory duties that an IMCA has to be involved in. But the response times to an instruction is a balancing act and ultimately needs to focus on the person. As previously stated, it is vital that timely referrals are made to the IMCA service so that they can fully represent the person, involve the person in the process and gather sufficient information from all those involved. From the moment it appears that IMCA involvement is required, a referral must not be delayed as this can hamper the due process that the person has a right to.

Report writing

One of the most important roles of an IMCA is to produce a report. This report must be sent to the decision-maker and must be used as part of the decision-making process. This report can prove invaluable in terms of advocating on behalf of the person, ensuring their wishes, preferences, and values are represented, as well as what decision they may make if they were able to. The report can also be used when highlighting concerns either about the decision-making process or the expected decision.

Again, Cowley and Lee (2010b) provide further detail on this subject in *IMCA Report Writing: Best Practice Guidance*, but the following is a useful reference.

By 2009 there was much variation with regards the layout of IMCA reports and so a template was produced not only to ensure there was more of a streamlined approach across all organizations that provide the service, but to ensure this acted as guide in creating reports that were person-centred as well as ensuring the conclusion provided an analysis of best interests using the evidence gathered.

IMCA Report

Client details	Decision details
Name:	☐ Serious medical treatment
DOB:	☐ Change of residence
Address:	☐ Adult safeguarding
	☐ Care review
Client ID:	

IMCA Caseworker	Date of instruction:
Service Manager:	Report no:
	Date report submitted:

Summary of decision to be made (including options being considered)
Decision maker:

Eligibility criteria
Outcome of capacity assessment:
Reason NHS/LA has deemed family/friends inappropriate to consult with (if applicable):

Actions undertaken by IMCA
☐ Medical records accessed
☐ Social care records accessed

The wishes, feelings, beliefs and values of the client

Information obtained (from discussions with people who know the client and written records)
Conclusion
Points for further consideration

This report is being sent solely to you as the Decision Maker in this case.

The Mental Capacity Act 2005 specifies that you are required to take this report into consideration when making the decision.

When the decision has been made, please complete and return the attached form by post or fax. In the meantime if there are any reviews/best interest meetings related to this decision please could you let the named IMCA worker on this case know.

Signed:

Date:

In 2013 and later published in the IMCA 2012/2013 Department of Health annual report, Empowerment Matters devised a report writing checklist. The aim of this was to enable commissioners to check the quality of anonymized IMCA reports from the service that they commission. IMCA providers equally have a responsibility to ensure their work is of high quality and is effective advocacy. It was felt this could provide an effective tool for both IMCAs and their managers to evaluate and monitor reports.

Following the report template and checklist will ensure that reports provide a true picture of the person, even in circumstances where communication or time spent with the person has been limited. All reports should end with a conclusion that, as already stated, provides an analysis of the best interests using the evidence gathered. This part of a report should make clear what the IMCA is advocating for based on this and most importantly the person's wishes. Where this is difficult to identify or the decision is so finely balanced it is not possible, then the conclusion should convey this and detail why this conclusion is reached.

The following are examples of conclusions and although these are very brief, should offer a sense of how an IMCA could conclude their work:

1. To conclude; as Jane's IMCA, I ask for serious consideration to be given to the option for returning home as this would reflect Jane's request, and her apparent view when she had capacity, given she had previously declined to live in a care home.

2. In terms of the best interests framework within the Mental Capacity Act 2005, the least restrictive option in this instance would be for Frank to return to his former residential placement; however, the nursing assessment has clearly indicated that his current needs exceed those that could be realistically met within a residential setting.

3. If this option were viewed as the appropriate decision I would advocate that consideration be given to the fact that Ruby is clearly stating she does not wish to be at home. Even with a full care package in place, this is not going to provide the type of environment that she is requesting. I would ask that considerable weight is given to her clearly expressed views.

Independent Mental Capacity Advocate Report Writing Evaluation Tool

EMPOWERMENT
matters

Commissioners may want to check the quality of the IMCA services they commission. IMCA providers have a responsibility to ensure that the work undertaken by IMCAs is of high quality and is effective advocacy.

Sampling IMCA reports (anonymised so that confidentiality is not compromised) can be a useful way of checking the quality of representation offered by IMCA services. Commissioners may also consider including the requirements for high quality IMCA reports in IMCA contracts.

The checklist can also be a useful tool for IMCA managers and IMCAs when evaluating the quality of IMCA reports in IMCA services.

General	✓
Is the report well written and does it conform to the IMCA provider's report template?	
Is the report person centred? Does it identify the client's wishes, feelings, beliefs and values? If this has not been possible, is the reason is stated?	
Are statements in the report clearly evidenced?	
Has the report been sent to the decision maker without unnecessary delay?	
Is the report evidence-based and balanced – has the IMCA looked at the pros and cons of each possible decision and included opinions from all those involved?	
Is there a conclusion that provides an analysis of best interests using the evidence gathered (balance sheet approach)?	
Reports should include	
Information from and about the person	
Details of what the client has expressed about the decision or any other information about what is important to them and how this has been established.	
Detailed information about the person's history that may give insight into the uniqueness of that person.	
A summary of the person's current situation, the decision to be made and how the decision will affect them.	
Information about the person gathered from records and people involved in the person's life.	
Actions the IMCA took	
People the IMCA consulted. Any quotes are attributed.	
Relevant information from the IMCA's research including information from CQC reports.	
Relevant details from the person's health and social care records that the IMCA has accessed.	
Details of any visits made to services e.g. prospective care homes.	
Anything else the IMCA is asking the decision maker to consider	
Alternative courses of action suggested by the IMCA.	
Issues not directly related to the decision that should be highlighted eg if the person needs ongoing advocacy.	
Any relevant case law.	
Particular aspects of the MCA that the IMCA wants to highlight eg if the person could be better supported to take part in the decision-making process.	

Empowerment Matters CIC
IMCA Report Writing Evaluation Tool
Advocacy and Mental Capacity Act Resource, Support and Information Agency
Liscard Business Centre 188 Liscard Rd Merseyside CH44 5TN 0151 203 5714 www.empowermentmatters.co.uk

4.   The IMCA report would usually outline the benefits and potential consequences of the proposed decision for a person. I have not done this in detail as I feel the best interests process has not been followed and would request that a move not occur until a review meeting takes place and Daniel afforded the right to an IMCA at the start of the process.

5. Initially it would appear from all the evidence obtained, for it to be in Sarah's best interests to have a CT scan and be sedated for this in order to provide an overview of what is occurring medically. However, I feel it is important to note that further medical environments/treatment, based on the evidence outlined within this report, would probably prove to be too distressing for Sarah.

6. If decision A is deemed to be in P's best interests, it is important to highlight that I would challenge this because...

7. A return home, even for a trial period, should be considered.

8. I have concerns that the LA are potentially not acting in P's best interests...

Impact of an IMCA report

One of the most public (and first) examples we've seen with regards to the difference an IMCA report can make is in the judgement of London Borough of Hillingdon v Steven Neary and others [2011] EWHC 1377 (COP). In examining the role of an IMCA it would be amiss to not refer to this valuable demonstrable difference as detailed below.

Steven Neary lives with his father Mark Neary. In December of 2009 he went to a respite unit earlier than planned due to his father's ill health. This was expected to be a short stay, but over a period of months Steven was prevented from returning home by Hillingdon local authority despite numerous requests by his father.

An extract from the Thirty Nine Essex Chambers Court of Protection Newsletter (June, 2011) summarizes the facts of the case:

> Steven initially went to a respite facility a little earlier than planned because his father was unwell and exhausted from caring for Steven over the Christmas period. His father wanted him to stay for a couple of days, but agreed to an extension of a couple of weeks; however, he expected that Steven would then return home. In fact, the local authority started a process of assessment of Steven's needs and decided that he needed to stay in the unit for longer, apparently primarily based on concern as to whether Steven's needs could be met at home even with support due to his behaviour, and on the fact that he had gained a considerable amount of weight while in the care of his father, most likely due to the use of food as a mechanism for managing Steven's behaviour.

The evidence before the court was that the local authority did not properly discuss its concerns or its plans for Steven with his father, and that Steven himself expressed a consistent desire to return home. No DoLS authorizations were granted until some four months after Steven had been kept at the respite unit.

www.39essex.com (2011)

In the following extract Jackson J summarized the IMCA report that was presented to the Court of Protection as part of the case:

The first *best interests assessment* that deserves the name *is the IMCA report* of 18 November 2010.

It is an impressive document. For the first time, professional support was given to Mr Neary's arguments. The previous best interests assessments are subjected to analysis.

The *IMCA's conclusion is that Hillingdon were potentially not acting in Steven's best interests* by refusing his father's request to have his son live with him at home.

The fact that *this is the most important relationship in Steven's life* was noted. No evidence had been presented to show that the care he had given to Steven over the years was no longer appropriate.

A return home, even as a trial period, *should be considered.* Further depriving Steven of his liberty might lead to emotional harm. Steven's wish to return home was rational and understandable and *Mr Neary had demonstrated in a number of ways his willingness to work positively* with professionals involved in providing care for his son.

This report pointed the way towards a different outcome for Steven.

Litigation friend

When a person is subject to proceedings within the Court of Protection they may lack the capacity to conduct the litigation themselves. In such a case a *litigation friend* must act on behalf of the person.

IMCAs carrying out the role of being a litigation friend is not a new concept; however, there has been an increasing demand and drive towards IMCAs carrying this out since 2012. This demand was partly driven due to two factors. First, the increasing strain on the Official Solicitor's resources (who acts a litigation friend in the following circumstances):

- As last resort litigation friend, and in some cases solicitor, for adults who lack mental capacity and children (other than those who are the subject of child welfare proceedings) in court proceedings because they lack decision-making capacity in relation to the proceedings.

- Acting as last resort administrator of estates and trustee.

- Acting as last resort property and affairs deputy in relation to Court of Protection clients

(justice.gov.uk 2014)

The impact of this meant that he couldn't act as litigation friend in cases in the way that everyone had anticipated when the Act came in. The second factor was an increasing feeling that acting as litigation friend was a natural extension of the IMCAs role, both of which led to IMCAs acting as litigation friends and seeking guidance as to how best to discharge their new role.

A Guidance Note on Litigation Friends commissioned by the Department of Health and written by Alex Ruck Keene, Barrister at Thirty Nine Essex Chambers and Honorary Research Lecturer at the University of Manchester was commissioned to enable more people, both IMCAs and others, to consider acting as litigation friends.

IMCAs may become litigation friends when they are involved already as the IMCA for the person and wish to progress the decision to the Court of Protection. Alternatively, IMCAs may be asked, by the local authority, NHS or the Court itself to carry out this role because there is no-one else willing and able to and the constraints on the Official Solicitor may mean the case is heard earlier than he is able to become involved.

What happens if there is not an IMCA available?
There may be times that the urgency of a decision in terms of timeframe available to make a decision means that an IMCA's availability is limited. IMCAs are not expected to be available in the case of emergencies of course, but there may be decisions such as serious medical treatment when there is only a window of a few days to carry this out. As previously stated IMCA services will usually have in place systems that enable them to get involved at

short notice where this occurs. Where this is not possible and a decision cannot be delayed, an instruction should still be sent to the IMCA. IMCAs may still be able to provide some representation, for example, by asking questions via email or telephone. They may have been involved with the person before and be able to provide pertinent information or a previous report that can be used as part of the decision-making process. Importantly they can also become involved in care reviews after the decision has been made.

Top tips

The following is a list of some 'top tips' to assist all those involved in decisions where an IMCA needs to be instructed.

- Timely instruction to IMCA services to enable them to carry out their role as effectively as possible and to ensure that the person's right to representation and support is not delayed.

- Include the IMCA (as well as the person) within informal (or formal) discussions or investigations, such as analyzing what is in their best interests. Merely to invite an IMCA to a best interests meeting where the above has already taken place is not in line with the expectation of the Act.

- Serious medical treatment decisions (the need to decide about providing treatment, withdrawing or withholding) is not about whether a decision is viewed as 'serious'. It is about the impact on the person which may include on their emotional, mental or physical wellbeing, their daily living activities, participation in society, independence, the need to restrain, sedate and so on. It is a holistic approach/criterion and not a purely clinical decision.

- If it appears that a person will require in-patient admission either to an acute hospital or mental health unit for 28 days or more (even where it is already believed that this is in their best interests, for example, rehab after a stroke) there is a duty to instruct an IMCA. The DoL safeguards may also become applicable.

- Where IMCA providers are looking to progress a case to the Court of Protection, it is important to note that challenging a decision remains the person's right. Where they are unable to fully exercise that right, it is the role of the IMCA to ensure that this is maintained. Commissioners must not be in a position of attempting to influence the IMCA to not fulfill their role.

Please note that the above omits the mention of the full criteria for instructing an IMCA (that the person lacks capacity and there is no-one other than paid staff appropriate to consult with) but this clearly applies.

Chapter 5

Advance Care Planning

The Mental Capacity Act emphasizes supported decision-making and enabling a person to make their own decisions where they are deemed to lack capacity. It also provides a framework for others to be able to make decisions on another person's behalf in their best interests.

But where the Act differs in comparison to other legislation where the focus might be very specific to one type of issue (for example, the Mental Health Act's focus is on those that are detained under the Act rather than those who have never been detained and there is no evidence to suggest they will be). The MCA applies to all of us, not just as a framework for others to make decisions on our behalf should we be unable to make them ourselves, but to allow us to plan in advance so that we are effectively making our own decisions even when we would otherwise be deemed to lack capacity.

The Act enables people that have capacity to prepare for a time in the future when they may know they are likely to be unable to make certain decisions. It also enables people to prepare even when there is no current evidence, whether diagnostic, medical or physical, that this will occur. It effectively allows us to prepare for the unknown as well as the known through:

- advance care planning
- advance decisions, and
- advance decisions to refuse treatment.

With this in mind it also enables professionals who work with a wide range of people to support them in carrying out any or all of the above.

A care plan in itself should be something that the person leads on, what they identify is important to them, and how they would like the care and support they're in receipt of to look like and this is usually focused on the short term, for example, to be reviewed once a month or once every three months.

However, advance care planning and to a degree advance decisions focus more closely on what is important to us and how this must be considered where a person might in the future be unable to articulate this themselves *or* put it into action.

The following offers an example of a situation where the unexpected happens. It can be adapted, but the essence of it remains the same, if something happened that means others had a level of control over your life: what would be important to you?

Example scenario

You are a professional athlete with a passion for extreme sports, including skiing. In two days' time you have a fall on the slopes and hit your head resulting in a massive brain injury. You are admitted to intensive care and as a result of your brain injury you acquire a number of physical and neurological impairments, which mean you are unable to communicate your wishes effectively with your family, friends, medical staff or other professionals.

If you know this is going to happen you can make arrangements to determine what will happen to you after the accident. These will obviously include some specifics, but will probably be based on a number of principles that could apply in different situations.

- Placing yourself in this situation and thinking about your own life, family home, and passions (be it work or in general) consider what is important to you.

- If someone didn't know you, would this information be freely available, e.g. through social media, friends/family, the décor of your house, hobbies, etc?

- Thinking about the number of decisions that would need to be made on your behalf for the future, how would you expect someone to ascertain what your wishes and views were if you were unable to express them?

The questions in the bulleted list are to make the reader consider not only how they might find out a person's previously expressed wishes, but in terms of advance care planning, introduce the idea of a person documenting what is important to them in their life. So for example, in everyday life, what is the person's routine; what *must* they have each day that's part of who they are; were a life-changing event to occur what would they want others to know about them?

The following are anonymous examples of what people have highlighted when this exercise is carried out in training and lists what they would want others to know should they go on to write an advance decision or statement of wishes:

- To be able to sit by a window each day and look out into the garden.

- To have a glass of port and listen to classical music each evening.

- I'd want my cats near me.

- I would not want a PEG feed.

- I think my mum would want me to live near her, but I left home such a long time ago, I'd want to stay here, where my home is now.

- I'd want a copy of the newspaper every day, it's my routine.

- My armchair, I'd have to have that, it's where I do my thinking.

- I wouldn't want cardiopulmonary resuscitation (CPR) performed on me.

Advance care planning should be person-centred and begin with a conversation about what is important to the person, who they are, their beliefs, their values and so on. Person-centered planning occurs predominantly in the learning disability field to ensure that there is a formal record for when new people may come into the person's life. It can be a record of conversations or interactions with the person. It can also be based on observations where the person is unable to communicate their wishes exactly, but it is evident they get pleasure from an activity, or alternatively where it is clear a person becomes distressed because of a medical intervention it can detail what is known to reassure them.

It can be difficult to focus on what actions a person would like carried out on their behalf, particularly in situations that they hadn't considered before or would choose not to. For example, care homes may find it useful to know whether the person would want to be resuscitated in the event this becomes necessary to consider, but this is a tricky subject matter to approach and there is no guarantee the person would have a clear view either way.

What can, however, begin to be recorded and gone through with the person is what they would like others to know as well as how they would feel if others had to make decisions on their behalf. Would they choose to nominate someone that knows them well to be a decision-maker through a Lasting Power of Attorney (LPA) for example, or would they find it beneficial to make a list of preferences?

This chapter does not aim to guide the reader to take a one-size-fits-all approach but rather to consider how they can work with individuals in a person-centred way where advance care planning might be useful for the person and/or others around them. Importantly, that advance care planning must begin with the relationship there is with the person; advance care planning can often be a deeply personal subject and therefore should not be viewed as an automatic 'care plan' that is carried out merely because a person is a client of a service or resident in a care home.

Lasting Power of Attorney

A power of attorney is a legal document that gives a person the opportunity to give someone else the authority to make decisions on their behalf. Attorney is the name given to the person appointed with decision-making powers within the LPA. Donor is the name given to the person that has made an LPA.

A court appointed deputy is where the court has appointed a person (it might be a family member, for example, or a solicitor) to make decisions on a person's behalf where they have been deemed to lack capacity.

There are two types of LPAs and Deputyships – personal welfare and property and affairs:

Personal welfare
Attorneys and/or deputies can be appointed to make decisions about personal welfare, which can include healthcare and medical treatment decisions. The person making the LPA will want to consider whether they want the attorney to be able to make life-sustaining treatment decisions or whether they give this responsibility to the relevant

medical professional. Personal welfare LPAs might include decisions about where the donor lives; day-to-day care; consent to treatment; who the donor can have contact with; medical, dental or optical treatment; assessments of care; personal correspondence; rights of access to personal information about the donor or complaints about the donor's care or treatment. This list is not exhaustive.

When attorneys are making best interests decisions they must consider the donor's past and present wishes, feelings, beliefs and values. Donors will want to ensure their attorney is familiar with these. Donors can appoint a deputy to make only certain decisions, for example, about social care, but not healthcare, or they may appoint different people for different aspects of decision-making. A personal welfare LPA can only be used at a time when the donor lacks capacity to make a specific welfare decision.

Property and affairs
Once registered, the attorney is allowed to make all decisions about the donor's property and affairs even if the donor still has capacity to make those decisions themselves. Alternatively a donor can state that the LPA should only apply when they lack capacity to make a relevant decision. Decisions may include buying or selling property, opening or closing bank accounts, receiving income on behalf of the donor, dealing with tax, rent, mortgage and household expenses, investing savings, paying for care, applying for NHS or social care funding, using the money to buy a vehicle or equipment or other help the donor needs. This list is not exhaustive.

(The above is a summary of what is laid out in the Code of Practice.)

Responsibilities and restrictions
Duties of attorneys

Once the attorney starts to act under an LPA, they must meet certain standards. If they don't carry out the duties below, they could be removed from the role. In some circumstances they could face charges of fraud or negligence.

Attorneys acting under an LPA have a duty to:

- follow the Act's statutory principles make decisions in the donor's best interests

- consider whether the donor has capacity to make the decision for themselves

- have regard to the guidance in the Code of Practice

- only make those decisions the LPA gives them authority to make

- apply certain standards of care and skill (duty of care) when making decisions

- carry out the donor's instructions

- not take advantage of their position and not benefit themselves, but benefit the donor (fiduciary duty)

- not delegate decisions, unless authorized to do so

- act in good faith

- respect confidentiality

- comply with the directions of the Court of Protection

- not give up the role without telling the donor and the court.

Restrictions on attorneys' powers

Attorneys are not protected from liability if they do something that is intended to restrain the donor, unless they:

- believe that the donor lacks capacity to make the decision in question

- believe that restraint is necessary to prevent harm to the donor, and the type of restraint used is in proportion to the likelihood and the seriousness of harm.

Attorneys have no authority to take actions that result in the donor being deprived of their liberty. Any deprivation of liberty will only be lawful if this has been properly authorized and there is other protection available for the person who lacks capacity.

Professional responsibility

Health and social care professionals need to be aware if someone else has responsibility for decision-making for a person and what specifically these responsibilities are. Where a person lacks capacity to appoint their own attorney, the Court of Protection can appoint a Deputy; the same rules and responsibilities apply to Deputies as they do to Attorneys. LPAs need to be registered with the Office of Public Guardian.

Health or social care staff involved in preparing a care plan for someone who has appointed a personal welfare attorney must first assess whether the donor has capacity to agree to the care plan or to parts of it. If the donor lacks capacity, professionals must then consult the attorney and get their agreement to the care plan. They will also need to consult the attorney when considering what action is in the person's best interests.

If healthcare staff disagree with the attorney's assessment of best interests, they should discuss the case with other medical experts and/or get a formal second opinion. Then they should discuss the matter further with the attorney. If they cannot settle the disagreement, they can apply to the Court of Protection. While the court is coming to a decision, healthcare staff can give life-sustaining treatment to prolong the donor's life or stop their condition getting worse.

(The above is a summary of what is laid out in the Code of Practice.)

Advance decisions to refuse treatment

The Code of Practice outlines in its chapter about advance decisions to refuse treatment (ADRT) one of the fundamental rights that people have with regards treatment decisions. This right remains even where a person is no longer capable of making the decision at hand:

It is a general principle of law and medical practice that people have a right to consent to or refuse treatment. The courts have recognized that adults have the right to say in advance that they want to refuse treatment if they lose capacity in the future – even if this results in their death. A valid and applicable advance decision to refuse treatment has the same force as a contemporaneous decision.

The Code also details what must be carried out when a person is making an ADRT when it is about life sustaining treatment:

An advance decision enables someone aged 18 and over, while still capable, to *refuse* specified medical treatment for a time in the future when they may lack the capacity to consent to or refuse that treatment.

If the advance decision refuses life-sustaining treatment, it must:

- be in writing (it can be written by a someone else or recorded in healthcare notes)

- be signed and witnessed, and

- state clearly that the decision applies even if life is at risk.

To establish whether an advance decision is valid and applicable, healthcare professionals must try to find out if the person:

- has done anything that clearly goes against their advance decision

- has withdrawn their decision

- has subsequently conferred the power to make that decision on an attorney, or

- would have changed their decision if they had known more about the current circumstances.

The key factor in making an ADRT is that they are about refusing treatment; they cannot be made in order to demand treatment. An advance decision must also be clear as to the specific treatment it refers to and whilst there is no requirement that a lawyer or a doctor reviews these statements once a person makes them, it would be fair to advise someone to have one or the other look at it. This is largely to ensure that whoever is making an ADRT is sure that what they have written down, expressed or wish is exactly how it will be interpreted by the treating clinician.

There is also no requirement for an ADRT to be written (unless it is for life sustaining treatment). What a person has verbally expressed to others, to their GP, articles they've written, poems, their lifestyle (for example, a person that actively chooses to not take prescribed medication, seek medical advice or believes strongly in homeopathy) must be taken into account.

However, for decision-makers the above can prove problematic in terms of how much weight is attached to past expressed views, questions may arise such as:

- Is there evidence or information that they may have changed their views?

- Did they make their views known where it is apparent they had not considered the current circumstances?

- Have there been advances in medical treatment that may have impacted on their views?

- Were they able to make the decision now, with full knowledge of their condition and possible treatment, would these views be the same?

- Did they view potential treatment as too invasive and there are now options that are less invasive?

- Did they have capacity at the time of expressing their views and wishes?

The above issues are a balancing act in terms of being able to come to a view about the validity and applicability of an advance decision where it is not written down. Where this considers someone that you may be working with who is considering making an advance decision, advice would be to treat it as if it were for life-sustaining treatment. That is, to ensure it is written down, for it to be witnessed and signed and to ensure it is accessible. For most people this will mean ensuring their GP has it on the person's records. Although there is a risk that a person still receives treatment for a few days when they have stipulated they would refuse (because contact with the GP is not immediate merely because a person is admitted to hospital) it will still ensure there is a formal point of contact where the GP can alert treating clinicians that an ADRT is in place and this be acted upon as soon as it's known about.

It therefore makes perfect sense for the person to let others know they have an ADRT, and to indicate this wherever possible (such as wearing a bracelet that stipulates this). Indeed many local authorities and ambulance trusts have in place systems (such as the issuing of cards that someone can carry on their person or an allocated place in a person's house) where they check for an ADRT.

Understandably there is a drive towards the making of advance decisions to ensure that should the situation arise the person has been able to make clear what their wishes would be. This negates the need for what can sometimes be drawn out best interests decisions because of the time spent attempting to ascertain a person's wishes and the level of uncertainty that this may carry. The impact of not having an advance decision, particularly for life-sustaining treatment, may be life-changing for the person as well as their family. In fact there are many organizations actively promoting the making of an ADRT, particularly with people where it is clear that at some point in the future they will lack the capacity to make some decisions. For example, a person with a terminal illness where CPR might be considered at some point, or dementia, where it is clearly evidenced by the nature of the disease that a person will lose capacity at some stage.

However, it is important to be cautious and sensitive in these situations. There are still many people who have not made an advance decision, people who are aware of what it is for and what it can do, but for whatever reason choose not to. It can be extremely difficult for any of us to plan that far in advance, to consider our own mortality. The fear of changing perspectives, views or decisions may hamper this (even though an advance decision can be changed or amended). Others prefer or choose for this decision to be driven by clinical expertise. In line with the Act this decision or the promotion of enabling a person to make this decision must be person-centred and done because they wish it, rather than for possible convenience or practicalities for those who may ultimately have to make a best interests decision on the person's behalf.

Advance decisions – Louise's story

In the following narrative, Louise Jessup who works as a mental health recovery champion and undertakes MCA training and consultancy work for a local authority and NHS Trust, explains how advance decisions within the construct of an advance care plan have supported her in her recovery and ongoing journey.

> I have a long-term severe and enduring mental health problem. Over the years I have seen different versions of advance decisions, the first in 2000 given to me by a very "clued up" social worker. It was suggested that I might like to fill one in as at the time I was becoming unwell with major depression about every 10 or 11 months necessitating hospitalization, increasingly being detained under the Mental Health Act.
>
> This first one was before the MCA and my social worker and I spent about an hour together when I was coming out of a bad spell looking at the things I wanted to happen should I become unwell again. Initially we discussed any treatment that I did not want and here I was able to discuss ECT and look at my reasons for not wanting it and agreeing a course of action should it

become necessary. I felt that having written and considered what I was refusing, I hoped that a doctor would respect my wishes and only use ECT as a last resort.

The other part of the making decisions in advance was in some ways more useful to me, as this was where I could write down my wishes and preferences about where and who should look after my animals and I could also think about how my house was taken care of while I was in hospital. I realized that an advance care plan and statement of wishes and preferences could be very useful documents if I worked through with the social worker as many practical things that I could, such as key holders for people who would look after the lighting and heating, someone to do the post and bring in the bills to me in hospital. A subsequent stay in hospital proved the worth of this early Care Plan and a lot of practical things were taken care of without me having to do anything extra, as people who were on the care plan to do certain things knew what they were doing, having been primed beforehand. This was a great relief for me, as I didn't have to worry about being away from home because it was all taken care of as planned.

In hospital the Advance Decision to Refuse Treatment was respected and although I was seriously unwell, they managed to treat me without ECT. With the introduction of the MCA and the "firming up" of the law around advance decisions, I embraced the new law to write a more up-to-date plan.

Although the advance decision stayed the same, with a refusal of ECT, I expanded the wishes and preferences section to have details of signs that things were deteriorating and what to do about them. When I became unwell the last time, the advance decision was picked up and together with the social worker we turned it into a very practical safety plan as well. This felt that I was taking ownership of my own risk and safety and helped me retain as much control of my own journey that I was able to at that time.

For me the advance decision is one of the most useful documents I have with a recurrent illness. It means that I am able to keep control of what happens to my basic needs and important things in my life even though I can be very unwell.

Although the advance decision that I use, as part of an advance care plan, is mainly for my mental health condition, parts of it, particularly the Statement of Wishes and Preferences, could be used if I became unwell for any other reason. I believe and hope that if my advance care plan is well considered and worked through, I will then have the confidence to get on with my life and not to worry so much if I become unwell. I would like professionals to embrace my advance care plan in the spirit of the writing of it and I hope they would respect my wishes as far as they can whilst helping to keep me safe and to become well again.

Advance decisions and the Court of Protection

The Court of Protection and judgments made there is a useful place to look with regards to advance decisions and the varying factors that have been considered in determining their validity and applicability. These judgments have carefully considered the person's wishes where either they could state what they were themselves or, where others in their lives knew them:

Case studies

Nottinghamshire Healthcare NHS Trust v J [2014] EWHC 1136 (COP) (Holman J)

J was a 23-year-old man, detained under the Mental Health Act. He had a diagnosis of serious personality disorder. A symptom of this was that he self-harmed to such a degree that it resulted in profuse bleeding. J had made an advance decision to refuse medical treatment, specifically blood transfusions. Significantly J was on anticoagulant drugs due to thrombosis and was also a Jehovah's witness; therefore his advance decision was a reflection of his religious belief.

This was an interesting case as it demonstrated the correlation between an advance decision made under the framework of the Mental Capacity Act that interlaced with the powers of the Mental Health Act. The judgement acknowledged that because J self-harmed due to his mental disorder, treating it could be justified and therefore lawful under the Mental Health Act. From an ethical perspective, J's treating clinician had rightly progressed this to the Court of Protection to ensure that both J and themselves had been afforded the appropriate safeguard to fully consider his capacity and decision by his psychiatrist to abide by it, even where this may result in his death. The outcome was that J had the capacity and that it would be an abuse of power to override this by using the Mental Health Act to treat against his wishes.

W v M and others [2011] EWHC 2443 (Fam)

M became unwell in 2003 with viral encephalitis, which left her with extensive and irreparable brain damage. Initially it was thought that she was in a permanent vegetative state (PVS). However, in the course of investigations, it was established that she was in a minimally conscious state (MCS) which meant that whilst profoundly neurologically and physically impaired, she still had some level of awareness. Her family after several years applied for a court order authorizing the withdrawal of clinically assisted artificial nutrition and hydration (CANH). This case was the first in this country in which a court has been asked to authorize the withdrawal of CANH from a patient in MCS.

M's family were of the strong view that she would not wish to be kept alive in her current state and offered several examples where she had indicated this when she had capacity.

The family's application was rejected and CANH was not to be withdrawn. The outcome raised some criticism namely due to the fact that Baker J stated:

> I accept the veracity of their (the family's) evidence, but I find that those statements were not specifically directed at the question that now arises, namely whether CANH should be withdrawn from her in a minimally conscious state, nor do I find that I can consider those statements as a clear indication some eight years on from the onset of her illness, of what M would now want to happen. Accordingly, while I take her earlier statements into account, I do not attach significant weight to them.

The criticism being that this appeared to be against what the Act values as important information to be considered when reaching a best interests decision (the person's previously expressed wishes). However, the rationale for reaching this conclusion is clear. Significantly, at the time, it made clear that an advance decision in these circumstances must specify the refusal of treatment when the person is in MCS. This too, however, attracted some criticism as it is not a widely well-known condition amongst the general population and therefore few people would actually do this; they may refer to a brain injury or even PVS, but not MCS because of a lack of knowledge as opposed to wishing for CANH to continue.

United Lincolnshire Hospitals NHS Trust v N (2014) EWCOP 16, (2014) MHLO 51

In 2014, however, a very significant judgement was made in almost identical circumstances as the above case where the person had previous conversations with loved ones when she had capacity that made clear she would not wish to be kept alive in these types of situations (but did not directly name MCS as one of those). Pauffley J summarized in his judgement:

> The critical decision is whether it is in N's best interests to continue invasive, risk-laden, medical care as would be involved in a further attempt at artificial feeding. I am utterly convinced that it would not. Accordingly, I declare that it is lawful and in her best interests for the clinicians (a) not to make any further attempt to secure a means of

providing artificial nutrition; (b) to withdraw the provision of intravenous fluids and dextrose; and (c) to provide such palliative care and related treatment (including pain relief) as considered appropriate to ensure she suffers the least distress and retains the greatest dignity until such time as her life comes to an end.

Whilst ultimately the outcome of WvM was not successful for her family or M (given they progressed what they believed M would have wanted, although this will remain unknown) However, this judgement paved the way for much progression in terms of guidance on the subject of prolonged disorders of consciousness (coma, PVS, MCS) which significantly formed part of future judgements made on this subject and where a person had expressed views about how they would wish to live (or not). All three judgements demonstrate the importance in determining either the person's capacity to have made an advance decision or what likely decision they would have made had they been able to make an ADRT. It is also worth noting that advance statements recorded on video can be a very useful tool.

Chapter 6

Best Interests

This chapter will consider the term 'best interests' and will focus on this within the context of a person who is deemed to lack the capacity to make a specific decision at a specific time.

It is important to note that the term 'best interests' is a term which pre-dates the MCA in that it constitutes an ethos of care which ought to underpin all care offered to all people in all situations. Historically, the term has different meanings for different people and as such has caused some confusion; for example, the term 'best interests' when used in a health care setting often specifically means what is in the person's clinical best interests, which is not the same as their MCA best interests. It is important that professionals are clear in their communication when they refer to what they believe is in a person's clinical best interests to others and that it is understood that this is only part of what constitutes MCA best interests. Health and social care professionals should always act in the best interests of the person who they are providing care and support to, but for the first time in law, the MCA offers a legal duty to act in the best interests of the person who lacks the mental capacity to make that decision for themselves.

The biggest issue we encounter within this process is whether individuals feel they have the competence to assess and determine what is in someone's best interests. It is suggested that 'competence' is not necessarily the issue, but 'confidence' is. Many professionals display their competence on a daily basis by engaging in the work they do with professional credibility and with the correct attitude that ensures that others receive safe, sound and supportive services. It's as if the work professionals do is unconscious, that they 'just do it' and in many examples this is all to the good. But when we have to justify our decisions, evidence how we have reached them and then go forth with authority given to us by law to enact them, then the confidence drops and we start to question whether we know what we're doing. Similarly, unconscious decision-making can encourage complacency in the decision-making process where clinicians simply do not consider the nature or degree of the actions which they are taking on behalf of P.

The MCA is aware of this and actually goes out of its way to support professionals and carers, but equally supports individuals to know that there is a legal duty within the MCA to ensure that their best interests should be identified and enacted. Admittedly, this all sounds good but in many respects it fails to identify what the key issue is and why, seven years on at the time of writing, the MCA is still not being adhered to nor fully embraced within practice.

This chapter will aim to look at what the stumbling blocks might be in practice and seek to provide a smooth path through them by demystifying what the MCA says about 'best interests'.

The question of all questions

How do I know what is in this person's best interests?

This is a question heard regularly up and down the nation in hospitals, care homes, hospices and day centres. It's a question that is easy to ask, but not necessarily easy to answer. The MCA does not provide a legal definition of 'best interests', not because it doesn't want to but because it is impossible to do so. The question is far too abstract to answer because what is in one person's best interests may not be what is in another person's best interests. The scope of making a best interests decision for someone is as expansive as people themselves, so asking the question, *'What is in this person's best interests?'* ought to be adapted to, *'Why does a decision need to be made in this person's best interests and what must be considered in order to achieve this?'*.

Section 4 of the MCA primarily considers 'best interests'; further guidance on this is contained within chapter 5 of the MCA Code of Practice. What the Act itself does is offer a checklist of what should and should not be done in order to make the best interests determination. There is an expectation that the person making that determination will make themselves aware of this checklist, so that they can say that they have done everything practicable and lawful in reaching their decision.

Previous chapters have discussed assessing capacity, maximizing capacity and advocacy so for the purpose of this chapter it will be assumed that we are discussing best interests within the context of the professional having made a determination that P lacks the capacity to make a specific decision. However, it cannot be stressed enough that we would only ever consider what is in another's best interests if we have evidence that P lacks the mental capacity to make that decision for himself. To override the decision-making and self-determination of a person who has capacity because of paternalistic and controlling cultures of care is abusive, and a contravention of that person's human rights.

Nothing within the scope of the MCA and the best interests checklist can override a person's human rights and there are exceptions to what decisions cannot be made in a person's best interests. Chapter 5.4 of the Code of Practice states clearly that a best interests decision cannot be made for someone who has previously made an advance decision to refuse medical treatment when they had the capacity to do so, nor can decisions be made in someone's best interests to be involved in certain research, to marry, to have a partnership annulled or to vote. None of these issues will be considered in this chapter, but what needs to be considered are those decisions which people, practitioners and carers experience in their day-to-day work and are decisions which are often made for P. Excluded decisions will be covered in more detail later.

When discussing the following I shall be reflecting on some of the work of the Kent and Medway MCA Local Implementation Network, particularly the guidance and suggestions of Annie Ho who is the MCA and DoLS lead for Kent County Council.

As mentioned earlier, decisions can be broken down into two distinct categories:

- Less complex decisions
- Complex decisions.

These terms are used in order to make reference to the processes which need to take place in reaching a determination which is usually measured by the complexity of who is consulted, who is involved in the decision-making process, how urgent the decision is and what the decision specifically involves. Ashton and Ward (1992) refer to a hierarchy of decisions that any person might make at any particular time. These are:

1. **Day-to-day living:** Quite fail-safe, no risk of something going badly wrong for the person if you make one decision or another. However, it can still be very important to get these choices right, for example, what to wear, where to go, whether to have tea or coffee.

2. **Activities with a degree of risk:** Day-to-day choices that involve more uncertainty but are vital if people are to develop personal relationships and independence, for example, going out alone, holidays, making friends.

3. **Major life decisions:** Where to live, who to have a relationship with, the spending or investment of large amounts of money.

4. **Major life decisions with legal implications:** Serious medical interventions, for example, sterilization or major surgery, financial decisions, for example, selling a property.

It could be suggested that very few decisions we ever make fall outside of these four categories, so as a rule of thumb it might be useful to draw an imaginary line between points two and three, and therefore suggest that decisions involving day-to-day living and those activities with a degree of risk (for example, crossing the road) are *less complex decisions* which any professional or carer might make for someone on an everyday basis with little awareness of the application of the MCA. As we move into points three and four, our awareness and accountability to the MCA and the person needs to increase and as a result confidence from the person delivering care or treatment can decrease in direct proportion, due to feeling intimidated by the perceived complexity of that decision. These decisions can be called *complex decisions*. The reason why the term 'perceived complexity' is used here is because that is exactly what it is. It may not actually be complex at all and the decision-making process, from the MCA perspective, is the same as if it were for a less complex, everyday decision. It is easy for clinicians to be become scared of the decision-making process and to delegate the task to another, but the process of reaching a decision in someone's best interests whether it be complex or less complex, is well set out within the MCA.

When making a decision in someone's best interests the starting point must always be the person and consideration of that person's wishes and feelings. Best interests decisions are *not* made by considering what you would want if you were that person, nor what others would want – even as family members. To remain focused on the person is the primary responsibility of the decision-maker.

Section 4(6)(a) of the MCA puts the needs and wishes and feelings of a person who lacks capacity at the centre of any decision-making process. The Code of Practice states that the person can express wishes and feelings about a particular issue:

- orally

- in writing

- through behaviour or habits

- plus expressions of pleasure or distress and emotional responses.

Combining the above with the requirement to consult with those who have an interest in the health and welfare of the person in order to engage them in the consideration of what may be in P's best interests can only serve to equip the decision-maker with the correct ethos and strengthen the quality of the best interests decision in addition to complying with the lawful requirements of the Act.

Chapter 5.38 of the Code of Practice states that the final decision must be based entirely on what is in P's best interests and discussing this openly and transparently with others will help to ensure that the entirety of the process of defining and concluding the outcome of this decision has been reached.

Case study: Less complex decision

Bethany has a learning disability and lives in a care home. Bethany's learning disability means she is unable to speak. Staff can often find it difficult to be fully aware of what Bethany is trying to specifically communicate, but staff try their best in getting to know Bethany, her family and those who know her well.

Bethany was recently diagnosed with diabetes and has put on weight which her GP said she ought to try and lose, as being overweight will exacerbate the symptoms of the diabetes.

Along with Bethany's family and consulting with the care manager, the care home staff developed a diet for Bethany with healthy food that she would enjoy whilst also managing to lose some weight. Bethany expressed no obvious upset at the diet change and still enjoyed an occasional treat whilst the staff remained mindful of her physical health needs and her preferences and wishes.

This is a *less complex decision* and although consultation took place with others and the process was recorded, the decision warranted little bureaucracy other than that.

Different circumstances warrant different levels of decision-making, and there will be times when professionals and carers need to be more robust in their decision-making processes because the decision is question may well have a bigger impact upon the person and be multi-faceted in the layers of involvement from others. Chapter 5.15 of the Code of Practice states that:

Any staff involved in the care of a person who lacks capacity should make sure that a record is kept of the process of working out the best interests of that person for each relevant decision, setting out:

- *how the decision about the person's best interests was reached*

- *what the reasons for reaching the decision were*

- *who was consulted to work out best interests, what particular factors were taken into account.*

The Code of Practice states that the record should remain on the person's file and that for major decisions it may also be useful for family and other carers to keep a similar kind of record.

What this suggests is that as the complexity of the decision and the potential impact on that person increases so there should also be an increase in the standard and amount of discussions, consulting with others and recording of processes. This is to ensure that P remains at the centre of the decision-making process and so that professionals and carers can be certain of their lawful and moral duty to remain mindful throughout of P's wishes and feelings (s4(6)(a)).

There may come a time when the decisions that need to be made for a person are deemed to be more complex in nature and degree and that there are many people who have an interest in P's life and circumstances.

In all but a few occasions, meetings are not welcome ways to spend time during busy days, but in these circumstances a meeting is the most efficient and helpful way to ensure that all reasonable steps have been taken to maintain P at the centre of the decision-making process. These meetings are often referred to by professionals as *best interests meetings*.

Best interests meetings

Best interests meetings are not actually referred to in the MCA, and therefore are not statutory meetings as such, but they do follow clear statutory processes and therefore ought to be considered as a formal meeting. Such meetings will take place when P has been assessed as lacking capacity to make a particular decision that is deemed to be more complex. In most cases best interests meetings are convened when considering a change of residence for P or consideration of medical treatment, but the decisions that warrant a meeting are fairly non-exhaustive and shouldn't be prescribed to specific landmarks or events.

It is important to note that a best interests meeting should only be named and considered as one if it has been convened to identify the decision that needs to be made on behalf of the person in their best interests (and make a decision where applicable, this may be done over a period of time rather than just in one meeting). For example, if a meeting is convened merely to relay what the local authority intends to do by way of care delivery, where the decision has been reached that a specific care package is to be delivered to the person on the basis that the LA considers that this is the option that properly meets the person's needs, and they are not offering any other (because they would be more expensive), this is not a best interests meeting.

A best interests meeting will usually be convened by the professionals involved or taking the lead in P's care, but there is nothing to suggest that family members nor P, through advocacy if necessary, may not call a meeting for themselves. The best interests meeting is the best and most reliable way to ensure that P remains at the centre of decision-making and that all those interested in P's health and welfare have an equal seat at the table. Earlier in this chapter competence and confidence was mentioned and when the term 'best interests meetings' are mentioned there can be a sense amongst professionals of concern and apprehension. If we view best interests meetings for what they are in a literal sense and familiarize ourselves with the best interests checklist in Chapter 5 of the Code of Practice then it is suggested that practitioner confidence will increase, due to the nature of best interests meetings becoming demystified.

Most local authorities, who take the lead in the implementation of the MCA, will have their own guidance on what a best interests meeting will look like and may even offer an agenda to guide the chair through the meeting. Such agendas are straightforward and should include:

Table 6.1: Agenda for a best interests meeting

Issue	Aim	Who
1. Welcome and introductions.	Information	Chair All
2. Apologies.	Information	Chair
3. Statements of confidentiality and equal opportunities.	Agreement	All
4. Clarify purpose of meeting: • Identify remit of decision to be made (does it need to be made today?) • State MCA 2005 as statutory decision-making framework. • Emphasize decision(s) to be made on the basis of what is best for P, not what they think they would make for themselves.	Information Agreement	Chair All
5. Confirm determination of lack of capacity in relation to decision(s).	Information	All

cont.

6. Is there any Advance Decision and/or other decision-making authority?	Information	All
7. Confirm name and role of decision-maker (person most involved in delivering care/treatment. Decision based on meeting's decision.	Agreement	All
8. Review of requirements of statutory checklist.	Discussion	All
9. Options and their potential outcomes. Discuss any risks and benefits.	Discussion	All
10. Selection of least restrictive option.	Agreement	Discussion
11. Risk identification and management.	Discussion and agreement	All
12. Dispute resolution.	Discussion and agreement	Chair and All
13. Summary of decision and proposed actions.	Information	Chair/ decision maker
14. Close of meeting.	Information	Chair

Source: Kent and Medway Local Implementation Network (2009).

Some best interests meeting agendas may ask that the decision to be made is clarified prior to the meeting. This is somewhat problematic as the decision is actually yet to be made (hence the purpose of the meeting) so to ascertain a specific decision prior to the meeting might render, in the mind of the cynic, the meeting to be tokenistic and just going through the motions.

The Chair of the meeting, after ensuring necessary introductions have taken place, ought to clarify the purpose of the meeting and what the decision is in relation to P. As suggested above, the paradox here is that at this point any capacity decision is decision-specific and time-specific, so the decision in question has, of course, been considered prior to the best interests meeting. What this doesn't mean is that professionals should have made their decision prior to the meeting. Failing to be open-minded within the best interests meeting and to not reflect upon all the issues and consult with others, whist remaining constantly mindful of P's wishes and feelings, would undoubtedly result in the spirit of the MCA not being applied and the statutory checklist not being adhered to. Therefore if we consider for a brief moment the decision-making authority that Lasting Power of Attorneys have by looking at the two types of LPA, then this can offer some guidance to seeking decision clarification at the start of the meeting. What this means is that at this point in the meeting the Chair should ask the person who undertook the capacity assessment what the decision is in relation to it being a health and welfare decision, or property and financial affairs decision. This at least offers some grounding to the start of the meeting by opening up options for the meeting to consider within the framework of the decision.

The Code of Practice states that the Chair of the meeting should not be the decision-maker. Again, we have a term here which causes much confusion and anxiety in that many professionals are reluctant to 'put themselves down' as the decision-maker. At this point, we should demystify this term a little.

Decision-maker

Chapter 5.8 of the Code of Practice asks the question 'who can be a decision-maker?' then proceeds to refer to various types of care given and the individuals who might be giving that to P. Looking at what the Code of Practice says the decision-maker can be summarized as the following:

Decision maker: The person delivering the care or treatment to P, relevant to that particular decision at that particular time.

This need not be made complicated, as many professionals and carers act as the decision-maker with all the authority and protection of the MCA behind them without even knowing that they are doing so, effectively undertaking this role within the eyes of the law. Professionals and carers have always acted as decision-makers for people who lack capacity to make certain decisions, and these decision-makers have, on the whole, always acted in P's best interests. So, again, the MCA is not specifically telling us anything new, other that formalizing a role that many have always been doing.

In less complex decisions, a best interests meeting will not usually need to take place because these are everyday decisions that might need to be made for P. Of course, this does not mean to say all due processes of ascertaining what is in P's best interests shouldn't take place, but it does say that professionals and carers ought to relax about this and be confident in the good person-centred care which they are providing.

In relation to a best interests meeting the decision-maker will have completed an assessment of capacity prior to the meeting taking place (see Chapter 3) and will have due regard to what kind of decision might need to be made for P. It is then the purpose of the meeting to discuss, debate and reflect whilst taking all practicable steps to ascertain P's wishes and feelings and the views of others, to reach a decision that the meeting believe is in P's best interests. The MCA does not say that the decision-maker must be certain that the decision is in P's best interests, but must have a reasonable belief on the balance of probabilities that it is. This reassures the decision-maker that the decision reached must therefore be more likely than not to be in P's best interests because all the circumstances, which they are aware of, indicate this.

For the sake of confidence and reducing anxiety, the decision-maker ought to enter the best interests meeting with the view that their role has been to assess P's capacity in relation to the decision and that they will be the person most involved in supporting P to carry through with that decision, *but* they are not making the decision themselves *per se* – the meeting is. The Chair ought to ensure that all parties present at the meeting know that they have equal responsibility in reaching a decision which is in P's best interests and that the role of the decision-maker is to simply carry that decision forward. Such an attitude not only supports the decision-maker with their confidence in the process, but also affirms family members/friends/carers and advocates that they have an equal place at the table and are central in the combined effort to act in P's best interests. There is often an unfortunate power dynamic in some best interests meetings, and this approach may go some way to help eliminate that.

The three-part plan

So, we know that by following an agenda and working our way through the best interests checklist we will be meeting legal requirements and the guidance of the Code of Practice in addition to the primary role of deciding the care and treatment that is in P's best interests. Some Chairs and attendees of best interests meetings remain unclear as to what a best interests meeting should 'look like' so what follows is a format (adapted from Ho (2009)) which is very clear but provides focus to the meeting whilst, again, aiming to demystify the process.

Part 1
Discuss current issues, risks and concerns in relation to P and work through the best interests checklist.

This is when all those present are offered a full and open opportunity to state their views, to have them heard and to have them recorded. These should be considered fully and openly with all parties having equal opportunities to discuss and reflect.

Once this has been done (of course bearing in mind that issues, risks and concerns can be discussed at any point in the meeting) then the meeting should work its way through the best interests checklist (below). It is important to remember that when working through this the meeting should be aiming to answer 'Yes' or 'N/A' to all the questions. This is not an arbitrary checklist (even though it might appear so!) but a mechanism by which to focus the meeting and ensure that the best interests of P remains at the centre of the decision-making process. In addition to ensuring that the decision-maker and those who are party to the decision-making process fully understand the process of making a decision in P's best interests, the checklist also offers the opportunity for those present to be prompted in relation to what needs to be considered in order to be satisfied that P's circumstances have been considered as much as is practicable.

The Chair of the meeting should guide the meeting through the checklist and prompt individuals to remain mindful of person-centred decision-making, which is exactly what the statutory checklist promotes.

Best interests checklist – Code of Practice, Chapter 5.

You must be able to assert that you have met the requirements of the Best-Interests Checklist of the Mental Capacity Act:

Have you avoided making assumptions based on the person's age, appearance, condition or behaviour?	Y...	N...	*Details*
Have you considered all the relevant circumstances?	Y...	N...	*Details*
Have you considered whether the person is likely to regain capacity and whether the decision can be delayed?	Y...	N...	*Details*
Have you tried whatever is possible to permit and encourage the person to take part, or to improve their ability to take part, in making the decision?	Y...	N...	*Details*
Have you considered your motivation in withdrawing life-sustaining treatment? (You must not be motivated by a desire to bring about the person's death.)	Y...	N...	*Details*

Have you considered the person's past and present wishes (expressed verbally, in writing or through behaviour or habits)?	Y…	N…	*Details*
Have you considered any beliefs and values (religious, cultural or moral) and any other factors which would influence the decision?	Y…	N…	*Details*
Have you consulted all relevant people as far as is practicable and appropriate to do so?	Y…	N…	*Details*
Have you considered other options that may be less restrictive of the person's right?	Y…	N…	*Details*

Source: Kent and Medway Local Implementation Network 2009.

Once, as a meeting, you have gone through this best interests checklist and satisfied yourselves through answering the questions and by discussing the details that you will adhere to these principles throughout the discussion, then you may move onto Part 2 of the meeting.

Part 2
Identify the options and weigh them up using the balance sheet below in relation to advantages and disadvantages.

Table 6.2: Balance sheet: a tool to help identify what is in P's best interests

	Advantages	**Disadvantages**
Medical	…	…
Emotional	…	…
Social Welfare	…	…

The balance sheet will help you consider 'best interests' beyond medical and or physical and to look holistically at P and his/her needs.

As the meeting progresses it may become clear as to what options are starting to be identified for P in relation to P's best interests. Advocacy and P's opinions are central and it is important to ensure that all options identified are considered against P's wishes and feelings and any advance decision made.

There will undoubtedly be meetings where carers or professionals arrive with a clear view as to what should be decided, and depending on the individual and his/her needs there might be only one or two probable decisions. Nevertheless, for each option identified complete the above balance sheet at the meeting. So, for example, if you have two options for someone – say, to remain in their own home or move into residential care, then you could complete two balance sheets (one for each option) which will help the meeting to express, but most importantly visualize, the options and their advantages and disadvantages. This helps to structure the weighing up process and clearly identify areas of risk and concern.

Discussing risks can be an emotive experience, particularly for concerned family members. It is necessary for all present to be able to express concerns, to have them noted and to be listened to and validated. From a constructionist perspective, 'risk' is subjective and risk aversion is an increasing trend being seen in practice. Understanding risk means that we should also understand paternalistic attributes which others can demonstrate when discussing risk. Few individuals will admit that such paternalistic views are expressed in order to oppress P, but it is quite natural that where risk plays a part in the life of someone who lacks mental capacity to make certain decision there will also be paternalistic views expressed as to how P should live their lives and what care should be given. Therefore consideration must be given to P's self-determination so as to ensure that the best interests meeting does not become a decision-making forum to suppress, and perhaps even oppress, P's rights, individuality and choices.

The best interests meeting is a partnership. It is a partnership between the person, family members, carers and friends, professionals and advocates. Trevithick (2012) states that the main concern that critics highlight in relation to the notion of partnership centres on the inequalities that exist in terms of power and control. This has been described as 'conflicting imperatives' with regards to 'rights versus risks, care versus control, needs versus resources, professionalism versus partnership with users, professional versus agency agendas' (Braye and Preston-Shoot 1995, p.63, in Trevithick 2012, p.264).

A best interests meeting is not utopian and does not offer what people necessarily want. Perhaps, most contentiously, they are not void of political agendas fuelled by agency resources and such issues may ultimately have an outcome on the decision of the meeting, but this does not suggest that the decision reached should be based on what is available at that time for the person. Similarly, the decision reached does not place a legal obligation upon a service provider to actually provide that service, but it does mean that whatever decision is reached must be reasonably believed to be in the person's best interests.

Chapter 6.32 of the Code of Practice states:

Carers, relatives and others involved in caring for someone who lacks capacity must have reasonable grounds for believing that their action is in the person's best interests. They must not simply impose their own views. They must be able to show that they considered all the relevant circumstances and applied the best interests checklist. This includes showing that they have tried to involve the person who lacks capacity, and find out their wishes and feelings, beliefs and values. They must also have asked other people's opinions where practical and appropriate. If somebody challenges their decision, they will be protected from liability if they can show that it was reasonable for them to believe that their action was in the person's best interests – in all the circumstances of that particular case.

Making a decision in someone's best interests is not a scientific process that has a concrete methodology attached to it, nor will any decision-maker be absolutely certain that the decision reached will be in the person's best interests. This may sound somewhat of a paradox but it is fair to suggest that certainty cannot always be achieved.

The only thing certain about certainty is uncertainty!

Of course, this does not suggest that ambiguity and lack of robust consideration of all the circumstances ought not to happen, but it does suggest that all that can be ultimately decided is that the best interests meeting has a reasonable belief that on the balance of probabilities the decision made is in P's best interests. This can generate tension within the decision-making process, purely because of its ambiguous nature. The Chair of the meeting therefore must reassure those present that the best interests checklist does not make the decision, but only provides statutory guidance as to what processes ought to be followed. This is when the 'balance sheet' can therefore come into its own by offering the meeting a clear opportunity to weigh up the potential decisions, discuss the tensions and risk and based upon a reasonable belief show confidence in deciding what needs to happen.

A simplicistic example of a balance sheet can be seen opposite (page 149). Mrs Adams is a fictional person and this balance sheet was prepared in a best interests meeting role play during a training course.

This balance sheet identifies the discussion that took place in relation to Mrs Adams either remaining at home (which was her wish) or residing in either supported accommodation or residential care. The case study tells us that Mrs Adams is 55, has a brain injury, is a widow, has no immediate family near to her and has recently been knocking on neighbours' doors at night in an agitated state. Within the training setting the scenario generated much debate in relation to risk and safety, but also her age and self-determination.

Part 3

Following discussion and working through the balance sheet it is necessary to define the decision that the best interests meeting is making. If this is a straightforward process and P's wishes and feelings are at the centre of the decision-making process then all to the good, but if there is disparity amongst the meeting then it is the Chair's job to permit further discussion time so as to essentially try and iron out those differences. Unless there is a designated lawful decision-maker already in place (such as a Lasting Power of Attorney or Deputy appointed by the Court of Protection) then it is important to note that no particular person can trump another in relation to making the decision. The decision-maker (as previously mentioned) is the person ultimately delivering the care or treatment or responsible for that person's care. Next of kin has no designated authority, albeit that there is a legal obligation to consult with that person. This means that the decision, by virtue of being next of kin, will not be theirs unless of course they are the person delivering the care or treatment or have specific authority to do so (LPA, appointed by the Court of Protection). The person delivering the care or treatment would therefore be the person who can ultimately make that decision and have the authority (as outlined by the MCA) to do so.

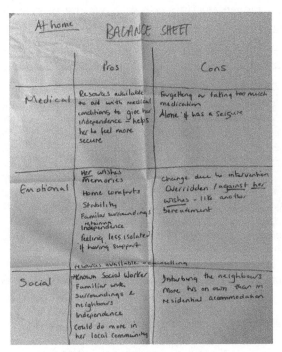

Figure 6.1: Example of a balance sheet

Just because you 'can' doesn't mean you 'should'!

Having authority within the scope of the MCA to make a decision in P's best interests does not give individuals carte blanche authority to make decisions because it feels the right thing to do. Nor does it suggest that moral obligation is about pressing ahead with decision-making whilst removing others from the consultation or decision-making process. The spirit of the MCA in this case is about enabling a best interests process that upholds P's human rights and will seek authority from a higher body if necessary.

If the meeting is unable to reach a decision and the decision is not of an emergency nature and can effectively wait, then it is suggested that mediation, the Public Guardian or the Court of Protection might need to be consulted. However, unless the decision is particularly complex, there is disagreement from other parties and is of urgency that a unanimous decision ought to be reached, then it is unlikely that the Court of Protection would be considered at this juncture.

The matter of Somerset County Council v MK Court of Protection judgement (July, 2014) is worthy of consideration at this point.

Irwin Mitchell Solicitors in their website release (September, 2014) stated:

In a judgement from the regional Court of Protection in Bristol which was published on 23 September, His Honour Judge Nicholas R. Marston found there were a series of 'systemic failures' by Somerset County Council which meant the 19-year-old woman, known only as 'P' for legal reasons and who was represented by Irwin Mitchell, instructed by the Official Solicitor as her litigation friend, was wrongly kept away from her family for over a year.

Irwin Mitchell says the case demonstrates the importance of ensuring all staff working within local authorities are given sufficient guidance and training about the Mental Capacity Act (MCA).

P, who has autism spectrum disorder and almost no verbal communication skills, was prevented by social services from returning to her family home in Yeovil in May last year following bruises to her chest being reported.

Despite teachers witnessing P's violent behaviour on a school trip, including hitting herself in her chest area, social services did not carry out thorough investigations, instead concluding that it was 'highly likely that P received significant injury from someone or something other than herself' and took the decision that she should not return home following a stay in respite care.

P was then kept in a respite facility in Yeovil for six months and sedated with medication despite her family's pleas for her to be allowed home. The local authority then moved P to an assessment and treatment unit after it was accepted that the respite placement was unsuitable, where she remained against her family's wishes until the case was heard by the Court of Protection.

www.irwinmitchell.com (2014)

This case clearly demonstrates that even though a local authority were of the opinion they were acting in P's best interests, it was certainly a case that P's family's 'pleas' to return home were not considered. It took the safeguarding process, which the Court of protection offers, for P to return home to her family which the Court declared was in her best interests. The concern which needs to be acknowledged here is that the Court of Protection is not just a facility which lawyers should be using on behalf of concerned individuals and family members who wish to disagree with a public authority's decision-making, but ought also to be a mechanism where the Court can be consulted on making the initial decision in relation to disagreement or concern encountered at the best interests meeting. Certainly, relatives and carers must be told about the Court of Protection and how it can be accessed.

Action plan
Once the best interests meeting has reached a decision which is in P's best interests, it is important that this is recorded as clearly as possible within an action plan ensuring that those present at the meeting know who is doing what and what the contingencies are (that is, stating that this plan will be reviewed in four weeks' time, for example). You must evidence clearly in the action plan that this decisions is:

1. In P's best interests.

2. The least restrictive option.

3. How you have involved P in the decision and in carrying it out (as far as is practicable and appropriate to do so).

Section 5 of the MCA provides protection from liability if the decision you have made is in the person's best interests. However, what is often not considered is that section 5 does not afford protection if the act in question is of a negligent or abusive nature. For example, using an amount of disproportionate force or making a decision that goes beyond the authority of the best interests process and ought to have been made by the Court of Protection. Therefore section 5 of the MCA does offer a level of support to the decision-making process by stating that clinicians and family members/carers should be confident of making best interests decisions but, in equal measure, they must remain mindful of the law, Code of Practice, and what case judgments clearly tell us. Even though many public bodies and individuals make decisions in good faith and without malicious intent, not applying the spirit of the MCA and being ignorant of its provisions will act as no defence when attempts might be made to justify unlawful decision-making.

As the meeting concludes, the action plan should form into a workable model of what needs to be done when and by whom and when, if necessary, a review of the decision might need to be made. The Chair of the meeting should ensure that no-one leaves with unasked questions and should give those present time at the end of the meeting to have points clarified. Minutes of the meeting should be sent out to all who attended.

This chapter has identified what might be considered as the difference between a *less complex* and *more complex* decision, the importance of consulting with others and when decisions may need to be taken to the Court of Protection. This chapter has also outlined what a best interests meeting might 'look like' when applying the *'three-part plan'*, but most importantly it is hoped that this chapter has gone a little way to demystify the perceived complexity of making decisions in P's best interests. In conclusion, those making decisions should not confuse the notions of competence and confidence. It is easy to fall into the trap of being intimidated by legal processes and to become paralysed by fear of applying the law. Equally to not abide by the principles of acting legally, morally and ethically in P's best interests due to arrogance and ignorance will lead to not only possible litigation but also to the more heinous offence of not placing P's best interests at the centre of the decision making process.

Excluded decisions
This chapter has discussed how the MCA offers provision for decision-makers to make a decision in the person's best interests. The MCA supports confident decision-making, but is clear also that if a decision can be delayed in order for the person's capacity to be maximized or for them to regain capacity (for example, after a head injury) so that the person is able to make a decision themselves, then this is what should be done.

However, the MCA does not support carte blanche authority for professionals/carers to make all decisions as there are some decisions that cannot be made in someone's best interests. The first of these is to provide treatment if you are aware that the person has made a valid and applicable *advance decision to refuse treatment*. This cannot be overridden as to do so would be akin to overriding the decision of someone who has mental capacity because you believe that you know what is their best interests. If there is concern as to the validity or applicability of an advance decision then you should seek clarification from the Court of Protection.

Sections 27–29 and 62 of the MCA set out the specific decisions which can never be made or actions which can never be carried out under the Act, whether by family members, carers or professionals, attorneys or the Court of Protection. This is summarized below from Chapters 1.10 and 1.11 of the Code of Practice:

- Consenting to marriage or civil partnership.
- Consenting to have sexual relations.
- Consenting to a decree of divorce on the basis of two years' separation.
- Consenting to the dissolution of a civil partnership.
- Consenting to a child being placed for adoption or the making of an adoption order.
- Discharging parental responsibility for a child in matters not relating to the child's property, or giving consent under the Human Fertilisation and Embryology Act 1990.

In addition to this if a person is detained in hospital under The Mental Health Act 1983 (amended 2007) and lacks capacity to consent to care and treatment the MCA does not authorize anyone to:

- give the person treatment for mental disorder, or
- consent to the persons being given treatment for mental disorder (this is because the Mental Health Act offers full provision).

Section 29 of the MCA does not permit anyone to vote, on behalf of the person who lacks capacity, at an election for any public office or at a referendum.

Section 62 of the MCA states that 'nothing in this Act is to be taken to affect the law relating to murder or manslaughter or the operation of section 2 of the Suicide Act 1961.' Basically this means that someone cannot be unlawfully killed or have their suicide assisted. This is certainly a topical issue as various organizations believe that to have one's suicide assisted is a fundamental human right if that person who has capacity makes an informed decision to do so and is suffering a terminal illness or debilitating condition, but at time of writing there is no lawful provision for this in the UK.

Chapter 1.11 of the Code of Practice refers to safeguarding vulnerable adults' provision by stating that although the MCA does not allow anyone to make a decision about these matters on behalf of someone who lacks capacity to make such a decision for themselves (for example, consenting to have sexual relations) this does not prevent action being taken to protect a vulnerable person from abuse or exploitation.

In concluding this chapter, we can see how the MCA enables practitioners to make decisions for people who lack capacity if they have taken all the necessary steps to ascertain what is in the person's best interests. Practitioners must remain mindful that the MCA has restrictions upon decision-making (above) and that any doubt of the decision in question or conflict being present amongst those involved in the person's care should propel others to seek legal advice and, if necessary, an application to the Court of Protection.

Nevertheless, the practitioner who seeks all opportunities to ascertain P's wishes and feelings, consult with others and adhere to the best interests checklist (as referred to in this chapter) is usually the practitioner who will not go far wrong and can hold their head high in relation to effectively applying the best interests checklist and making it real and beneficial for the person who lacks capacity.

Chapter 7

Liberty and Choice

This chapter will consider liberty and choice within the context of the spirit of the MCA as discussed throughout this book. Liberty is a central tenet of UK law and underpins good practice within care homes, hospitals and care within people's own homes. We must support people to make decisions and assert choices within the care and treatment they receive and the MCA upholds people's rights to make those decisions, even if they might be deemed to be unwise by others.

When liberty and choice is discussed we must ask ourselves on what authority we are acting to impose (and quite often care is imposed!) our views and decisions upon others. The MCA offers safeguards that are libertarian in content inasmuch as they defend the liberty of people who might lack capacity. But equally the MCA also offers the safeguards to restrict and deprive people of their liberty should this be absolutely necessary in their best interests to protect them from harm. This clearly presents tension in practice and concern from individuals and their families because no-one wants to have their liberty limited or removed, but sometimes there may be no other options available to safeguard that person. The paradox of whether restriction/deprivation of liberty actually gives people more rights and upholds good standards of care will be discussed.

Nevertheless, having said this, restrictions or deprivations of liberty that do not adhere to the MCA and are not in P's best interests will be unlawful. The key issue might be whether care staff actually know they are acting unlawfully in the provision of their care, or whether such actions have come about because of the culture of care in that organization.

In very simplistic terms restriction of liberty means to *limit* and deprivation of liberty means to *take away*. These considerations will be useful when helping us to understand later in the chapter what might constitute a restriction or a deprivation of liberty.

This chapter will first discuss 'restriction of liberty' within the context of choice and people's self-determination and then the discussion will focus on deprivation of liberty, what this means in relation the DoLS – the deprivation of liberty safeguards.

Restriction of liberty

When reflecting upon restricting liberty we must first consider why we should never restrict people of their liberty, and when we do that we have very clear reasons for doing so. Yet again, we ask the question on what authority am I acting in this situation? Everyone has the freedom to make decisions, choices, express opinions and live their lives in the way they see fit, including what care people wish to accept or decline. The only time this liberty can be contained or removed is if law states so because of a risk of harm to self or others, or because of other parameters stated by law within the context of caring for others in their best interests. Some examples of this are:

- Criminal justice – imprisonment, for example.

- The Mental Health Act 1983 – detention for assessment and/or treatment.

- The Deprivation of Liberty Safeguards – which this chapter discusses.

- Parental responsibility under the Children Act 1989 – where a parent (or other person with parental responsibility) has the authority to make decisions for children under the age of 18, noting that if the child is the age of 16 or over then the principles of the MCA apply. The only difference is that the decision-maker for a 16- and 17-year-old who lacks mental capacity due to an impairment or disturbance in the mind or brain, will be the person with parental responsibility.

There are other examples of when law can remove freedoms, but these will not be discussed in this chapter. What is important to note is that care professionals must have an awareness of how they are making decisions for people and on what authority they are acting should there be any indication that another's liberty is at risk of being restricted or deprived because of such actions.

The concept of restriction of liberty is somewhat of a paradox. By restricting someone's liberty in their best interests, we are not seeking this action to remove the person's rights nor to oppress that person, but because the agenda for such action is to prevent harm, to establish safe-care and to perhaps actually offer that person more liberty because through the care offered they can access greater opportunities.

Case study

Nick had a head injury at the age of 24 following a motorcycle accident. He lives at home with his parents and receives care from them with the help of his siblings and professional carers. Nick is mobile, but is impaired somewhat and he is prone to stumbles and falls. Nick can make most decisions for himself but sometimes lacks the capacity to understand the risks involved in going out alone. By using a wheelchair and by being taken out he can access those things which he enjoys doing, but his liberty is restricted somewhat by having others with him.

Nick's mum and dad, Mark and Alison, need to strike a balance between supporting Nick to make decisions but by also making decisions, in his best interests, to have someone with him when he goes out. Mark and Alison do not seek to restrict Nick's liberty but by occasionally doing so he is able to have more experiences whilst being safe within those experiences.

When considering 'restriction of liberty' within the context of the MCA we need to look at the Act itself and seek a definition of what it actually means. The MCA refers to 'restraint' when referring to restriction of liberty. What we are not referring to here in this chapter are concepts of 'control and restraint' when techniques may need to be used to subdue people, but we are referring to restraint in relation to restricting the liberty of someone who lacks capacity in that person's best interests.

Section 6.4 of the MCA states that someone is using restraint if they:

- **use force** – or threaten to use force – to make someone do something they are resisting, or

- **restrict a person's freedom of movement,** whether they are resisting or not.

'Force' is not defined in the MCA nor the Code of Practice but could constitute a carer guiding P back to their care home, a paramedic holding someone's arm down who is confused and disorientated in order to receive care or treatment. It could also be staff preventing P from inflicting harm upon themselves.

Section 6.4 is not so much giving practitioners permission to go ahead and start restraining people, in fact on the contrary. It offers guidance around what is lawful if it has to be used in exceptional circumstances. The spirit of restriction of liberty is to focus on liberty and only consider restricting that if there is no other way to act in P's best interests.

As with force, 'restricting a person's freedom of movement' is not defined. But what practitioners could imagine here is what this might look like when it occurs in care settings. A classic example would be to 'keep an eye' on someone around the care home every now and then due to risk of falls or undertaking an activity that may cause harm to themselves.

Action point

At this point in the discussion, care providers are encouraged to reflect upon reasons why they might need to use force to care for someone or restrict that person's movement and to consider this by looking again at Chapter 1, 'Culture of Care' and Chapter 4, 'Advocacy and Empowerment'. A question that care home managers and owners and hospital managers could ask is, 'What is it about my service that could propel someone to act in a way that causes us to have to use force or restrict their liberty?'

Staff resource issues, lack of access to outside activities, boredom, not getting on with certain staff or peers, illness, effects of medication and difficulties with communication (to suggest only a few) can all be reasons as to why people act or react in certain ways. The MCA does not support force or restriction of movement being considered when attention should be given instead to looking at the reasons why people might need to be brought back to a care home or prevented from leaving. This is a key issue and it is suggested it ought to be a key imperative in how services are managed and delivered.

Who decides?

Capacity and adulthood are concepts of great importance when reflecting on who can make the decision around someone's care.

There is so much mythical practice 'out there' that it is worth considering for a moment.

A story was recently heard of a care home who sought permission from a service user's relative around access to community resources and the spending of amounts of money over a certain limit (prescribed by the relative). Alternatively, a story was also heard of a care home where the service users fully decided what they spent their money on, what they did and when. Any information being passed onto relatives about this was viewed as a breach of confidentiality.

There are two myths within the care profession that seem as alive and well now as they have ever been, these myths are:

Next of kin

True or false: A person's next of kin (spouse, civil partner, son, daughter, parent, for example) can make decisions for their loved one if that person is unable to make a decision for themselves.

False. In English and Welsh law 'next of kin' has no legal definition and merely refers to who you consider to be your nearest and dearest; this may be stipulated in law by marriage, for example, or under the Mental Health Act 1983 (amended 2007) in relation to that person having certain rights, *But* your next of kin has no legal authority to make decisions in your best interests if you lack capacity unless that person:

- has been given legal authority to do so by section 4 of the MCA as your *decision-maker* because they are delivering your care and/or treatment

- is a donee of a registered Lasting Power of Attorney (and the decision falls within the scope of that specific LPA)

- has been appointed by the Court as a Deputy to make decisions for you within the scope of authority given by the Court.

Of course, being a next of kin for someone is important in that they may be consulted with in relation to decisions, but asking P's next of kin to make decisions for them or for permission to act in a specific way is unlawful practice, because that person has *no* authority to do so solely by virtue of being next of kin.

Common law doctrine of necessity

Basically, this is when a person believes it is necessary to either break a law (whether criminal or civil) in order to undertake any act of great necessity or emergency (for example, breaking into a building to rescue someone in a fire). In relation to caring for people who lack capacity and if there is urgency to act in P's best interests, this 'common law' mostly does not apply. Many professionals still refer to *doing the right thing because it's an emergency,*' but the MCA offers full provision to act in P's best interests. The MCA refers to acting in P's best interests to protect harm from themselves, but Chapter 6.43 of the Code of Practice states that is it lawful to *take appropriate and necessary action'* under common law to restrain or remove someone who lacks capacity if they cause harm to others (or themselves) because of their lack of capacity.

In the first chapter of this book, when considering *cultures of care*, we looked at Mandip's story and what care home staff did in relation to his best interests by restricting his liberty to leave the care home until extra staff were present to take him. As mentioned in that chapter the question that care home staff need to ask themselves is, *'on what authority am I making this decision?'* There is no place in modern, person-centred care to railroad over people's choices and decisions and to care for them in ways that are akin to the least favourable elements of parental care. When we objectify people we have a problem. This often results in controlling and paternalistic care or care that infantilizes adults, often resulting in dependency upon the care-giver due to autonomy and self-determination being gradually chipped away.

Degree, intensity and frequency

In Mandip's situation what happened did not amount to a deprivation, but a proportionate and reasonable restriction of liberty to safeguard him at that time. Mandip was restricted because he lacked the capacity to understand the risks involved in going to the shop on his own and it was in his best interests to wait until someone could go with him. Only on this occasion was Mandip not free to leave. At all other times he is able to go out without restriction and nothing in his care plan suggests he is under continuous supervision or control, or not free to leave.

The 'acid test' in relation to the DoLS is clear that if the care being offered to Mandip constituted *continuous* supervision and control and Mandip was not free to leave the home then restriction of liberty could no longer be justified and a DoLS authorization would need to be made. Therefore it is imperative that all care staff remain mindful of the care that is being provided, when it might amount to controlling care and the degree, intensity and frequency of safeguards that are being implemented. This should be recorded clearly, be transparent amongst the care team and full risk assessments undertaken.

Liberty must always be promoted and there are times when restricting or depriving someone their liberty will not be permissible under law and therefore be an unacceptable act. Conversely, not restricting the liberty of someone who lacks capacity when it would be clearly in their best interests to do so in an urgent situation could be an act of omission leading to a safeguarding concern and perhaps concern that the member of staff had willfully neglected P, which is a criminal offence under section 44 of the Act. An example of this could be not preventing a vulnerable person who lacks capacity from leaving a hospital or care home when the outcome of their leaving is likely to be catastrophic; the same applies to returning that person to a care home, if returning them to the care home is in their best interests and the act is proportionate to the harm being experienced or likelihood of harm occurring to that person.

It is clear to be seen that tension does indeed exist when considering this issue. Confidence in what the MCA tells us and applying this to any given situation that may arise will support practitioners to reflect on law, but most importantly, have the rights of P at the centre of their decision-making.

There are examples of cases where restraint under the MCA has been used unlawfully. One of these, for example, is *R (Sessay) v South London and Maudsley NHS Foundation Trust (2011) EWHC 2617 (QB)*, known as the Sessay case. To put this very simply, this was when the police entered a woman's property to take her to hospital due to her mental health needs and because it was felt to be in her best interests. The police suggested they were acting under sections 5 and 6 of the MCA and therefore restricting her liberty in her best interests. She was removed to hospital and kept there for 13 hours until she was detained under the Mental Health Act for assessment. This was unlawful simply because the Mental Health Act 1983 (amended 2007) offers full provision for the care and treatment for people who experience mental health difficulties, including powers for police to enter premises under a warrant and for someone to be assessed at home and conveyed to hospital. The MCA cannot be used to do things 'to' people just because they appear to lack capacity and require care or treatment. In the Sessay case the MCA was not appropriate because the Mental Health Act would have been adequate, and it is that legislation that the police and mental health services should have considered and used to not only meet the healthcare and safety needs of this person, but to also safeguard her rights and protect themselves in ensuring their actions were justified and lawful.

Protection from liability

Section 5 of the MCA works very much in conjunction with section 6, in that section 5 states that practitioners will not incur liability in relation to their actions if they can justify they have a reasonable belief that P lacks capacity and the act is in P's best interests. Of course, practitioners will not be protected from liability if they show negligence in undertaking the act. Similarly, if provision to meet that person's needs is offered in the Mental Health Act 1983 (amended 2007) then this is the course of action that should be taken.

An example of this is that if a carer puts up a bed rail believing P cannot consent to that act due to lack of capacity and it is in P's best interests to have the bed rail up then the carer will be protected from liability, unless a negligent act occurs.

Similarly, paramedics who use reasonable and proportionate restraint, including sedation, to convey someone who lacks capacity to hospital and who is resisting, following a road accident, will be protected from liability unless that act demonstrates negligence (for example, knowingly ignoring a valid Advance Decision to Refuse Treatment (see Chapter 5)).

Chapter 6.2 of the Code of Practice also helps us to understand this:
Section 5 of the Act provides 'protection from liability'. In other words it protects people who carry out these actions. It stops them from being prosecuted for acts that could otherwise be classed as civil wrongs or crimes. By protecting family and other carers from liability, the Act allows necessary caring acts or treatment to take place as if a person who lacks capacity to consent had consented to them. People providing care of this sort do not need to get formal authority to act.

As we looked at (above) section 6(4) of the MCA offers us the legal definition of restriction of liberty. Care providers ought to remain mindful of the following when considering care plans that involve restrictions of liberty being considered when delivering care in P's best interests:

- Human Rights Act 1998 (ensuring that P's fundamental human rights are not breached – for example, people's rights to a private and family life and freedom of expression),

- People should decide and control their own care and be treated with *respect* and *dignity.*

- A culture of care that embraces full risk assessments, least restrictive action, recording of decisions, regular reviews and seeking advocacy services for those who have no family and friends.

- Person should be fully involved in all decisions about their care and if they lack capacity, someone should act on their behalf.

- Inappropriate use of restraint is against the law – can constitute assault, battery or false imprisonment and can lead to criminal prosecution.

(*Ho 2009*)

'We're not allowed to restrain people'

There appears to be a fundamental concern present within care organizations in relation to restriction of liberty; this is usually encapsulated in the statement that was heard often on MCA training courses – *'We're not allowed to restrain people.'*

This was a statement that generated much debate and required much deeper and wider thinking. It usually warrants an initial response of, 'Well, why would you want to?' This statement is often expressed because care providers view any restriction of liberty as something negative and involving hands on 'restraint'. It's a taboo subject in many care homes and hospitals which is a problem because not discussing it as a concept and as a part of care provision leads not only to the formation of myths, but a lack of understanding and confidence of, sometimes, essential good practice.

Forms of restriction of liberty for people who lack capacity are common and often necessary practices in care agencies if used for the right reasons. Some examples of these might be bed rails in the hospital setting and in care homes, belts for wheelchairs, and locks on kitchen utensil cupboards. Therefore, to suggest restraint is 'not allowed' is not only a non-statement because it is in fact being used (you just don't realize it's being used) it also implies someone else has to authorize or allow restraint to happen. Guidelines are helpful, but any use of a restriction of liberty, such as a bed rail, should be incorporated into the person's care plan with a full risk assessment and, where appropriate, consultation with others. However, the ultimate decision lies with the care-giver at that material time, as it is he or she who is responsible for delivering the care or treatment for the person who lacks capacity and therefore has the authority of the MCA to deliver that care in the person's best interests if the criteria for a restriction of liberty are met.

Making a distinction

There will be times when a distinction needs to be made in relation to whether care decisions amount to a restriction of liberty or deprivation of liberty. Of course there will be times when someone is unrestricted, but knowing when a restriction of liberty might amount to a deprivation of liberty is key in this equation.

A restriction of liberty

May include factors that do not amount to a DoL, but restrict movement such as temporarily locking a ward, taking a patient back to a care home who has left in a confused state, or use of benign force.

A deprivation of liberty

May include the use of force or sedation to take a resisting patient to hospital or to prevent a patient from leaving, the use of subterfuge, a decision to admit to hospital being opposed by relatives/carers and of course the 'acid test', as referred to in this chapter.

Good practice suggests that carers should be asking questions when delivering care and treatment in order to remain mindful in relation to issues of liberty, choice, restrictions and deprivations of liberty.

Consider all the circumstances of each and every case and ask yourself...

- What measures are taken in relation to the individual?
- When required? What period?
- What effects on the individual?
- Why necessary?
- What aim?
- What views of relevant person, their family or carers? Do any of them object?
- How are the restraints/restrictions implemented?

(Ho 2009)

Any deprivation of liberty that is occurring or is likely to occur (having carefully considered the above and the 'acid test' in relation to care in hospitals and care homes) must be lawful, and each organization must seek legal advice if there is any doubt in relation to this.

Section 4A of the MCA discusses restrictions (or limitations) on deprivations of liberty and, essentially, *prohibits* deprivations of liberty occurring so that people's rights to liberty and choice are upheld. However, there are three occasions when the MCA permits deprivations of liberty in order to act in a person's best interests. These are:

1. Under the *Deprivation of Liberty Safeguards (DoLS)* of the MCA (known formally as Schedule A1 – more about this later in the chapter.)

2. When the *Court has made an order* under s16(2)(a) of the MCA for someone to have their liberty deprived in order to receive the care they need. This, for example, could be authority for a relative or carer to deprive someone of their liberty in their own home in order to deliver essential care in the person's

best interests, if they lack capacity. DoLS cannot be used in this case because the safeguards do not currently apply to people's own homes or supported accommodation. In the case of care or treatment for mental disorder in someone's own home (for example, dementia) the Mental Health Act 1983 (amended 2007) will undoubtedly offer more suitable provision for that person's needs if deprivation of liberty is required.

3. Under *section 4B of the MCA*, where a decision-maker (carer, for example) is authorized to deprive a person of their liberty (under this section) 'for the purpose of providing him with *emergency medical treatment for either a physical or mental disorder* while a decision as respects "any relevant issue" is sought from the court.' (Jones 2012). If the Mental Health Act 1983 (amended 2007) ought to be used as this offers the provision which the person needs then they would be ineligible for this third option in relation to treatment for their mental disorder. This third option is essentially, authorization to deprive someone of the liberty in order to deliver emergency, life-sustaining treatment whilst a decision is waiting from the court.

If when delivering care or treatment to a person, evidence suggests the care being delivered amounts to a *restriction of liberty* (i.e., the three points above are not relevant) then section 6 of the MCA may be applied if a restriction of liberty is necessary, but this must NOT amount to a deprivation of liberty.

Legal criteria for restraint

(MCA section 6 and Code of Practice, chapter 6)
P lacks capacity and it will be in P's best interests; *and*

- it is reasonable to believe it is necessary to restrain P to prevent harm to them *and*

- the restraint is a proportionate response to the likelihood of P suffering harm and the seriousness of that harm.

When these criteria are met, the restraint must be:

- the *least practicable amount of force*

- for the *shortest time possible*
- used according to *agreed guidelines*
- a *last resort*: other methods tried, unsuitable or failed
- an urgent action only to be used in exceptional circumstances.

The above criteria do not offer carte blanche authority for carers to start restraining people in order to managing certain 'behaviours' or to justify ensuring care is delivered in the way the care organization wishes to deliver it. In essence, the question to work back from in determining whether a restriction of liberty should be imposed is to consider whether or not there is an emergency and the person is likely to experience significant harm if they were not to be restrained. It is therefore important to consider that the least likely risk of harm, and the least likely restraint should be considered. The rule of thumb is thus:

1. Restraint (restriction of liberty) is only to be considered if P, because of a lack of capacity, is likely to experience harm and there is no other way to safeguard P or act in P's best interests. (For example, running out into a road or needing to be taken to hospital in a confused and uncooperative state, or being prevented from leaving a care environment due to safety concerns.)

2. Restraint (restriction of liberty) is *never* to be used to assert control or authority over P in order to provide day-to-day care.

3. If P is subject to continuous supervision and control and not free to leave your care home or hospital, then a DoLS authorization is required.

It is encouraging to see care organizations that seek all opportunities to get to know well those who they provide care to. Ethics and values run through the centre of 'restraint' like letters through a stick of rock. Care homes, hospitals and carers in people's own homes ought to consider constantly the reasons why restraint may need to be used… and why it should not. The term 'challenging behaviour' is one that might say more about the organization or person saying this term than the person to whom it refers. Who is being 'challenged' by this 'behaviour' and what do we even mean by 'behaviour'?

If we reflect upon our own actions, personality and ways in which we communicate, we might use other adjectives to describe ourselves, such as 'assertive', 'confident', 'enabled' or 'upset', even 'exasperated'. But yet, there is a pervading sense of recipients of care being referred to as 'challenging'. Perhaps, it might be a case that practitioners are challenged by the person's self-determination, expression of autonomy or difficulties in communicating their concerns or upset. Therefore to gain a deeper understanding of the people we provide care to can only serve to help us deliver care in the least restrictive way possible. Training and professional development will also help is gaining these understandings as staff embrace new cultures of care and seek to understand laws, policies and principles of good practice.

Chapter 5 of the Code of Practice refers to consulting others; it is therefore necessary to discuss any restrictions of liberty with family members and carers in order to seek their views on the least restrictive options for care. Undoubtedly, family members will have views on this and may guide professionals on how best to meet their family member's needs.

A sound ethos of care and, in particular, in relation to restraint is required. The culture or care should be one that will only consider using restraint in an emergency to protect P from harm, and to develop safe and sound practice.

Finally, a key consideration in relation to restrictions of liberty must always be based around concepts of degree, intensity and frequency (as discussed earlier). Knowing when a deprivation of liberty is occurring, rather than the one-off urgent restriction of liberty, is central in lawful, reflective practice. Knowing when to consider applying for a DoLS and doing so in a person's best interests is a sign of a safe, sound, and supportive service.

Deprivation of liberty and the safeguards
The Deprivation of Liberty Safeguards came into force in April 2009 and were introduced into the MCA due to a 2004 European Court of Human Rights ruling known formerly as HL v UK 45508/99 (2004) ECHR 471 (or HL v UK), but this judgement is mostly referred to as the 'Bournewood Judgement'.

This judgement evidenced a legal loophole in UK law whereby many vulnerable adults were being detained unlawfully in hospital and care homes. This loophole was known as the 'Bournewood Gap'. The 'gap' was closed in 2009 by the introduction of the Deprivation of Liberty Safeguards (DoLS).

When the MCA was first implemented in 2007 there were guidelines about Deprivation of liberty, aimed to act as a trigger or guide to identify where a deprivation of liberty was occurring. These were based on the HL v UK judgement and where a deprivation of liberty was identified then the provisions of care and treatment needed to either be changed, that is, to ensure that there was not a deprivation of liberty *or* if it was deemed to be in the person's best interests and there was no other way of providing appropriate care and treatment without depriving the person of their liberty, this needed to be progressed to the Court of Protection.

Deprivation of Liberty Safeguards Code of Practice

Though these safeguards were mentioned in the main Code (particularly in chapters 6 and 13), they were not covered in any detail. That was because, at the time the main Code was published, the deprivation of liberty safeguards were still going through the Parliamentary process as part of the Mental Health Bill. The Mental Health Bill was used as a vehicle to amend the Mental Capacity Act 2005 in order to introduce the deprivation of liberty safeguards. The Bill became the Mental Health Act 2007 following completion of its Parliamentary passage.

The DoL Safeguards were intended to ensure that the Court of Protection was not overwhelmed by applications when it was deemed that the Local Authority or NHS could effectively authorize the DoL. This was of particular importance due to the volume of people that have a mental disorder, who lack capacity to consent to their care and treatment, leading to deprivation of liberty, it being deemed to be in their best interests to protect them from harm. The safeguards do not apply to those detained under the Mental Health Act as there are sufficient provisions within this Act to provide care and treatment; but were intended as a legal safeguard and framework for where the Mental Health Act does not apply, including for those who may be a patient in a mental health unit but as an 'informal' patient.

The safeguards apply where the person is in an NHS hospital, care home or private hospital registered under the Care Standards Act 2000. For all other living arrangements the decision needs to be authorized by the Court of Protection. As previously referred to the managing authority (NHS or care home – whoever is responsible for providing the care and treatment at the time the person is in either environment) has the responsibility in identifying where there is a deprivation of liberty. They must seek authorization for the DoL from the supervisory body (local authority for where the person is ordinarily resident – where the person is not ordinarily resident in that local authority, the supervisory body is the local authority where the care home or hospital is).

Where a third party (such as an advocate including IMCA, other professional or person involved in the persons care) identifies or has concerns that there is a deprivation of liberty occurring that has not been authorized, then they must raise this with the managing authority. Third party referrals may also be made to the supervisory body, for example, where concerns have been raised with the managing authority but no action has been taken.

There are six assessments that must be carried out:

- **Age assessment** – to establish if the relevant person is 18 or over.

- **Mental capacity assessment** – to establish whether the relevant person lacks capacity to consent to the *arrangements* proposed for their care or treatment (carried out by anyone eligible to act as a Mental Health Assessor or Best Interests Assessor (BIA)).

- **No refusals assessment** – to establish whether an authorization for DoL would conflict with other existing authority for decision-making for that person (carried out by anybody that the Supervisory Body considers has the skills and experience to perform the role).

- **Eligibility assessment** – to establish whether the relevant person should be covered by the MHA 1983 of DoL under

MCA 2005 (carried out by the BIA or someone familiar with the Mental Health Act if this is not the same person).

- **Mental health assessor** – to establish that the relevant person is suffering from a mental disorder within the meaning of the MHA 1983 (carried out by a doctor that is approved under Section 12 of MHA 1983; or Registered medical practitioner who has special experience in diagnosis and treatment of mental disorder and has completed appropriate MCA 2005 mental health assessor training).

- **Best interests assessment** – to establish first whether a DoL is occurring or is going to occur and if so whether it is in their best interests, that it is necessary to prevent harm to themselves and the DoL is proportionate to the likelihood and seriousness of the harm (carried out by the BIA).

These six assessments are carried out under the two DoLS' authorizations which are the actual structures which provide authorization for Managing Authorities (care homes and hospitals) to deprive a person of their liberty and for that person to have the legal safeguards provided to underpin, govern and oversee the authorization. These authorizations are known as an *urgent authorization* and a *standard authorization*.

A managing authority must request a standard authorization when it appears likely that, *at some time during the next 28 days*, someone will be accommodated in its hospital or care home in circumstances that amount to a deprivation of liberty and meet the requirements of the acid test. The request must be made to the supervisory body which is the local authority of where the person is being accommodated. The only exception to this is when the managing authority would be the authority which is funding the person's care in a residential care home setting. In this case the managing authority would approach that local authority. The managing authority will need to ask for the team which manages DoLS authorizations. In some local authorities this is quite simply known as 'the DoLS office'. Whenever possible authorization should be obtained in advance, if the person's care plan, for example, indicates that the person is likely to be deprived of their liberty soon or where the person is going to a hospital or care home and is likely to require a DoLS being in place when they get there. The only exception to this would be if the person requires care and treatment for a mental disorder in hospital and requires detention – the Mental Health Act 1983 (amended 2007) will offer full provision for this.

Where this is not possible and the managing authority believes it is necessary to deprive someone of their liberty in their best interests before the standard authorization process can be completed, the managing authority must itself give an urgent authorization and then apply for a standard authorization within seven calendar days (see Chapter 3.4 of the DoLS Code of Practice) (Ho 2009).

An urgent authorization can never be given without a request for a standard authorization being made simultaneously. Therefore before giving an urgent authorization a managing authority will need to have reasonable expectation that the six qualifying requirements for a standard authorization are likely to be met (see Chapter 6.1 of the DoLS Code of Practice) (Ho 2009).

So, in summary:

Standard authorization

- Planned request that will be required within the next 28 days.

Urgent authorization

- Managing Authority gives it to itself (person is being deprived of their liberty now and is unavoidable. A Standard authorization should always be sought at the same time).

Important for care homes and hospitals to remember...

The DoLS process can seem very complicated and even a little intimidating for care home and hospital staff to fully understand. The above discussion gives a brief insight into what the authorizations 'look like' and the obligations of managing authorities when considering DoLS.

The bottom line of all responsibility, however, is that care home and hospital staff must *not* ignore the DoLS process because of its apparent complexity, but must first and foremost identify if anyone in their care (1) has a mental disorder and lacks the capacity (because they have been assessed to lack capacity) to consent to the arrangements made for their care and treatment; (2) is under *continuous supervision* and (3) *control* (all three elements must be met) and is not free to leave. If these requirements are met then the managing authority, if in any doubt whatsoever, *must* pick up the phone and consult with either their MCA/DoLS lead (many hospital Trusts have these) or the local authority DoLS office or DoLS/safeguarding team. By picking up the phone and making contact you are embracing the spirit of the Mental Capacity Act and of DoLS and will be commended for doing so.

Responsibility to instruct an Independent Mental Capacity Advocate (IMCA)

There are three distinct IMCA roles within the safeguards. The numbers and letter refer to the section of the MCA that legislates for the IMCA's provision.

39A IMCA

An IMCA must be instructed during the assessment process, where there is no-one appropriate to consult (other than paid staff) to support and represent a person either when there is a request for a standard authorization or when a best interests assessor has been appointed to establish whether there is an unlawful deprivation of liberty.

39C IMCA

Once an authorization is in place, the relevant person should be appointed a representative known as the 'relevant persons representative' (RPR). This is normally a family member of friend, or where there is no-one able or willing to carry out this role then a paid representative must be appointed. Many IMCA services also provide the paid representative role although local authority commissioning arrangements may vary.

Sometimes there will be a gap in the provision of this role, for example, the RPR becomes unwell or goes away for a lengthy period of time and is unable to continue with the role. Where this gap in representation occurs then a 39C IMCA must be instructed.

It is important to note that the role of a 39C IMCA must not be used where there has been a failure to appoint a representative, that is, they must not be instructed to fill the gap because the authorization process has not identified a family member or friend. Should this occur then a paid representative must be appointed; the role of the 39C IMCA only becomes applicable when, for whatever reason, the appointed representative is unable to carry out their duties.

39D IMCA

Must be instructed when the person is deprived of their liberty and an authorization is in place and either they or their unpaid RPR (relevant person's representative, who could be a family member or friend) request the support of an IMCA. The role here is to support either party during the authorization process. This may be to assist with understanding as to what an authorization means and what their rights are, for example, a right to a review or to make an application to the Court of Protection. The IMCA may also request a review or apply to the Court of Protection. The Supervisory Body must also instruct a 39D IMCA when it believes either the person or their representative may benefit from this support.

An unpaid RPR is not expected to be an expert on the Mental Capacity Act or Deprivation of Liberty Safeguards and it is for this reason that the 39D IMCA role was created to ensure there is additional independent support and guidance for the RPR.

The Department of Health and subsequent guidance has recommended that the Supervisory Body instruct a 39D IMCA automatically to enable the person and/or their representative to make an informed choice as to whether they would benefit from this support. Anecdotal evidence suggests this does not always occur and many RPRs state that they were not even made aware that they could access a 39D IMCA.

The role of the IMCA in DoLS

SCIE Guidance *IMCA and paid relevant person's representative roles in the Mental Capacity Act Deprivation of Liberty Safeguards* (SCIE Guidance 41, 2014) list the following as to what an IMCA will want to consider when carrying out their role and submitting their representation on the person's behalf:

39A IMCA

....

- Is there a deprivation of liberty?
- Are the restrictions in the person's best interests?
- Conditions (the IMCA may suggest conditions or respond to conditions the best interests assessor has recommended).

- Duration (the IMCA may suggest the length of duration or respond to the best interests assessors recommendation).

- Person's representative (whether the IMCA has a view as to who this should be).

- Mental Capacity Assessment (whether the IMCA has a view on the person's capacity or concerns about this part of the process).

Roles 39C and 39D which are about supporting the person and/or their representative may include discussing the above, addressing concerns or challenges made by the person as through a review process. For example, conditions may not be being met or the person is distressed about the restrictions.

The IMCA involved in all three roles may been part of previous decisions (such as accommodation, treatment or safeguarding) and therefore may know the person better than others involved in the person's life, offering them further opportunity to comment on the above.

Bournewood

The following account of events is written by Mr and Mrs E and HL, and describes their experience including the legal challenges made that resulted in HL v UK and which ultimately ensured that deprivation of liberty and all its safeguards became enshrined within the Mental Capacity Act.

Bournewood – Where it all began

We were first introduced to HL in December 1993 as part of a resettlement scheme for moving patients from long stay hospitals into the community. We were given very little information about him and we were not told he was autistic. A difficult induction period followed, caused by organizational mismanagement, but in March 1994 he eventually moved in.

He was completely institutionalized, head bowed, hands clenched, shuffling, unable to walk through an open doorway without being given permission to do so, no social skills at all and with no personal possessions to accompany him. HL, as well as being profoundly autistic, does not speak, but with prompting he learned to communicate using eye contact and body language. He began to hold his head high, unclench his fists and walked with a spring in his step. Everyone was amazed by his remarkable progress.

HL should have been fully and formally discharged from the hospital within six months. However, the organization responsible for the resettlement programme, the hospital and social services were engaged in conflict over how the programme was managed. The regime we were expected to work to was stifling and controlling and didn't allow Harry to have any choices at all. Everybody had to conform. By June 1994 our relationship with the organization had deteriorated to such an extent we expressed our concern to the hospital managers. Following an investigation, the hospital terminated the contract with the placement organization. This resulted in the other seven placements being returned to the hospital, but because of his outstanding progress HL remained with us.

However, it was out of the frying pan and into the fire. We were still stuck with the same psychiatrist who appeared to resent the fact that HL remained with us. The promised contract with the hospital never materialized and the psychiatrist refused to formally discharge him. By October 1996 the social services involvement was about to be withdrawn and we were warned that there was a real possibility that the clinicians would readmit HL. However, by July 1997, after months of liaising behind the scenes, we had finally reached agreement with the health authority and social services that HL was to be formally discharged into the community, much to the displeasure of the psychiatrist.

On 22 July 1997 transport arrived to take HL to the day centre he was obliged to attend by the hospital. On this day there was a different driver who took a different route picking up more people, making the journey longer. The last person onto the bus was very disruptive and upset HL, who became very agitated.

At the day centre, the situation was badly managed and the hospital psychiatrist sent an ambulance to collect HL and take him back to the hospital where he was drugged and immediately admitted to the severe behavioural unit.

We were not allowed to visit – the psychiatrist wrote *'We do not wish to face the scenario that HL would expect to leave with you'* and in her contemporaneous notes, *'Afraid the E's will come and remove H'*.

HL's care manager was told his admission would only be for a couple of days, but it very soon became clear that the psychiatrist had her own agenda. Representations made by HL's GP, MP, Social Services, Health Authority, Mencap, National Autistic Society and of course ourselves were all fobbed off by the use of the phrase – *clinical decision*. The psychiatrist wrote to the Health Authority, *'The least favourable option would be to send him home to his carers.'*

It was clear from our daily conversations with the unit manager that HL was deteriorating. The unit manager expressed his concern and kept saying, *'We don't know why he is here.'*

In early September 1997 we had received a letter from the hospital stating HL's stay would be a prolonged one and effectively ending HL's placement with us. We were unable to find a high street solicitor to take on HL's case, but Mencap found us a specialist London solicitor who we met on 18 September. He was sceptical at first, but as he read through the bundle we had presented him with he became more and more incredulous at the actions of the psychiatrist and stated that he believed we had a case.

Within days a barrister had been appointed and an application made to the High Court for Judicial Review and writ of *Habeas Corpus* heard on 25 September with a hearing dated listed for 3 October. We lost the case and were initially refused leave to appeal, but a day or so later leave to appeal was granted. Legal aid had not been granted by the time of the Appeal Court hearing on 29 October. The Court suggested an adjournment to see whether a suitable third party could achieve reconciliation.

HL's solicitor said it was 'do or die', no legal aid agreed – if we went ahead and lost the case it would be the end, that is, do the case now or maybe not at all. We said go ahead. At 5.30 pm Judges rule HL is detained and his detention is unlawful. In their verbal judgement at the time they said that either HL meets the criteria for being detained under the MHA 1983 or the hospital must let him leave. In spite of this the hospital immediately sectioned HL even though the emergency duty team referral form states the doctor's 'opinion is that HL doesn't meet the criteria for section 3'. The Chief Executive of the hospital said it was to protect their legal position.

At 9.00 am next morning while HL's social services care manager was on the phone making arrangements to collect HL, a fax came through informing that HL had been sectioned. However, this did give HL some rights – visitors, independent assessment, access to a mental health review tribunal and to hospital managers. Our first visit was blocked by the hospital with the excuse of not enough staff to supervise.

When we did get to visit, because of the shocking condition we found HL in, we kept a diary. Contrary to the hospital's submissions to the court, HL was detained in a locked ward. *HL was unrecognisable; he looked haunted, anxious and struggling against medication. He was extremely dishevelled and had not had his hair cut for some time. He had lost a considerable amount of weight and was not wearing any of his own clothes. He was agitated, pacing and bashing his head, which was bleeding, there was blood on his hands, clothes, the walls and the door.*

During the next month the controlling clinicians demonstrated an inability to listen to the views of other professionals from the health authority or the hospital director and took no apparent notice of the independent assessment commissioned for a Mental Health Review Tribunal, which recommended HL's immediate discharge back to his home with us.

At a meeting on 4 December the clinical staff were still being obstructive about Section 17 leave when at the end of the meeting the hospital director informed them that following receipt of a letter from HL's solicitor he was putting the staff on notice that there would be a Managers' Review in order to discharge HL from the Section. The clinical staff then reluctantly agreed to the Section 17 leave and HL came home the following day.

We returned to hospital on 12 December for the Managers' review. The Approved Social Worker (ASW) didn't recognize HL in his own designer clothes and he had already regained half a stone of the weight he had lost and was calm and smiling. Hospital staff wanted HL to wait on a ward while the review took place. We refused, saying HL should attend. The review lasted less than 10 minutes. HL was discharged fully and finally from hospital. The responsibility for HL's care moved to new health area.

February 1998 – Care manager made a complaint to hospital about the state HL was in on his return home and the way he had been mistreated in hospital. Police investigation came to nothing because HL was unable to say who inflicted his injuries. The police left the hospital to investigate themselves.

February 1998 – Department of Health lodged appeal to House of Lords.

HL appears on Newsnight the week before the House of Lords hearing 25 June 1998 – although the case was lost it was the dissenting judgement from Lord Steyn that caused the most attention identifying a 'fundamental gap in our mental health law'.

Lord Steyn House of Lords, June 1998

In my view 'L' was detained because the healthcare professionals intentionally assumed control over him to such a degree as to amount to complete deprivation of his liberty.

Referred to again in ECHR 2004

Any suggestion to the contrary was fairly described by Lord Steyn as *'stretching credulity to breaking point'* and as a *'fairy tale'*.

September 1998 – Formal complaint to hospital by HL's solicitor. Complaints procedure not resolved until November 2001 with NHS Ombudsman Report upholding our complaint stating that HL should have been discharged back home on the same day and at the very latest the following day.

December 1998 – case to ECHR.

May 2003 – hearing in Strasbourg.

October 2004 – ECHR judgement in HL's favour – sets up path for legislation changes to close the 'Bournewood Gap'.

January 2006–2008 Under the Safeguarding procedures we asked for an Independent investigation into professional abuse. The hospital trust refused and instead we were obliged to accept a serious case review – the main criterion being 'not to apportion blame'.

April 2009 – Deprivation of Liberty Safeguards.

Definition of deprivation of liberty

Cheshire West

The history that surrounds the Cheshire West Judgement is summarized as follows.

It involved two separate cases that were heard in the Court of Protection, which later went to the Court of Appeal and following this, both cases were heard in the Supreme Court.

P&Q v Surrey Council

P&Q (also known as Mig and Meg) were two sisters who had learning disabilities and became the subject of care proceedings in 2007. Prior to this they had lived with their mother and stepfather where they had been neglected and ill-treated. Mig, aged 18, lives in a foster home where she had resided since being taken into care and Meg, aged 17, had not settled in a foster home and so lived in an NHS care home. In 2008 their care orders were transferred over to the Court of Protection. Their case looked at issues of contact with family, and whether either living situation required a deprivation of liberty authorization. Both were under continuous supervision, neither tried to leave their accommodation and both seemed relatively settled. In the first judgement Mrs Justice Parker deemed that neither were deprived of their liberty. The Official Solicitor appealed and when the case was heard in the Court of Appeal it also determined that they were not deprived of their liberty.

Cheshire West and Chester Council v P

In this case a young man with cerebral palsy (P) and Down's syndrome lived in a small group home. P was incontinent and had developed a habit of tearing off pieces of his incontinence pad and putting them in his mouth. He had a very detailed care plan that included how to manage this, but he also wore an all-in-one body suit that zipped at the back as a further safeguard. He had intensive hours in terms of the number of 1:1 support, and there was no question as to whether these arrangements were in his best interests. In the first judgement, Justice Baker considered the fact that P was under continuous supervision and deemed that he was deprived of his liberty and that it was in his best interests. However in the Court of Appeal judgement, Munby LJ deemed that P was not deprived of his liberty as the factor of 'relative normality' had not been taken into account.

What was similar about both judgements was something that became known as the 'relative normal comparator' or 'relative normality'. In essence this meant that when considering if someone is deprived of their liberty, you cannot compare them to someone:

> With the life of the able-bodied man or woman on the Clapham omnibus, but with the kind of lives that people like X would normally expect to lead. The comparator, in other words, is an adult of similar age with the same capabilities as X, affected by the same condition or suffering the same inherent mental and physical disabilities and limitations. (Munby J)

In effect what this meant was that if a person has severe disabilities to the point that their disability restricts their freedom of movement, their choice and their actions, then their environment or the care they receive cannot be considered one of a deprivation of liberty. The person's level of disability and need in itself already does this and that by simply changing their environment, this would not alter their circumstances.

The judgments also highlighted that there was not a query being posed about the suitability of the environment, or the care arrangements, indeed it was recognized that all three were accommodated in their best interests.[1]

---

1   To access the Supreme Court judgement which contains details of both cases: http://supremecourt.uk/decided-cases/docs/UKSC_2012_0068_ Judgment.pdf, accessed on 3 December 2014.

Supreme Court Decision

P (by his litigation friend the Official Solicitor) (Appellant) v Cheshire West and Chester Council and another (Respondents)

P and Q (by their litigation friend, the Official Solicitor) (Appellants) v Surrey County Council (Respondent)

The two cases were heard in the Supreme Court in October 2013 and the judgement was given on 19 March 2014.

Lady Hale highlighted in terms of whether a deprivation of liberty required authorization that:

> It is no criticism of them if the safeguards are required. It is merely a recognition that human rights are for everyone, including the most disabled members of our community, and that those rights include the same right to liberty as has everyone else.

In response to the idea that when looking at whether there is a deprivation of liberty, there needs to be a comparator between characteristics of similar disabled people, Mr Richard Gordon QC, instructed by the Official Solicitor stated that:

> *This confuses the concept of deprivation of liberty with the justification for imposing such a deprivation. People who lack the capacity to make (or implement) their own decisions about where to live may justifiably be deprived of their liberty in their own best interests. They may well be a good deal happier and better looked after if they are. But that does not mean that they have not been deprived of their liberty. We should not confuse the question of the quality of the arrangements which have been made with the question of whether these arrangements constitute a deprivation of liberty.*
>
> *An unconscious or sleeping person may not know that he has been locked in a cell, but he has still been deprived of his liberty. A mentally disordered person who has been kept in a cupboard under the stairs (a not uncommon occurrence in days gone by) may not appreciate that there is any alternative way to live, but he has still been deprived of his liberty. We do not have any difficulty in recognizing these situations as a deprivation of liberty. We should not let the comparative benevolence of the living arrangements with which we are concerned blind us to their essential character if indeed that constitutes a deprivation of liberty.*

Lady Hale emphasized this:

> ... *But, as it seems to me, what it means to be deprived of liberty must be the same for everyone, whether or not they have physical or mental disabilities. If it would be a deprivation of my liberty to be obliged to live in a particular place, subject to constant monitoring and control, only allowed out with close supervision, and unable to move away without permission even if such an opportunity became available, then it must also be a deprivation of the liberty of a disabled person. The fact that my living arrangements are comfortable, and indeed make my life as enjoyable as it could possibly be, should make no difference. A gilded cage is still a cage.*

Lady Hale asked whether there needed to be an 'acid test' for these types of cases and if so what was this? And in a detailed judgement, Cheshire West, has provided and clarified the test to determine whether a deprivation of liberty is occurring.

The new test for deprivation of liberty

1. The person lacks capacity to consent to their deprivation of liberty (the regime/care which constitutes the deprivation of liberty); and

2. The person is 'under continuous supervision and control and ... not free to leave' their placement, and

3. The care regime is 'imputable to the state'.

What stands out within this judgement is the clear comparison with the final judgement in HL v UK in 2004 and it is the second point that led to many questioning how the judgements (or the 2nd judgement in the case of Cheshire West and Chester Council v P) could have ever led to the view that neither party was deprived of their liberty.

The Supreme Court decision has now ensured that there is a clear definition and thus has ensured that all practitioners are working within the same framework. Prior to this it meant that in one local authority the assessment process could deem that a person was not deprived of their liberty; yet in another with exactly the same circumstances an authorization was approved. This inconsistency in practice and interpretation of the law was clearly something that needed to be addressed and whilst it has understandably resulted in an overwhelming increase in authorizations, which in itself impacts on resources across the board, it does mean that equality in recognition of 'P' has been achieved.

What this means in practice

Within the existing DoL safeguards that apply in care homes and hospitals, an assessment must occur when the above three points apply. With regards to supported living arrangements, any authorization must still be heard in the Court of Protection.

But who will this apply to and what does it actually mean in practice? Points 1 and 3 are relatively self-explanatory, but it is point 2 that has left some practitioners querying what this means. For example, where the person is enabled to go out from the care home with a member of staff, this has been interpreted as the person is therefore free to leave. But this is not always correct; this is 'free to leave with conditions', whether these conditions are the availability of another person, permission of another person or funding that enables it. Therefore the test is clear and must be applied as intended.

The new test will and has seen authorizations for people that are in a permanent vegetative or minimally conscious state, in a hospice, that have been discharged from a section of the Mental Health Act (and where the framework of the MCA applies) amongst others. It remains an ongoing development both in terms of practice, resource availability and future guidance.

Current DoLS practice issues

This chapter will conclude by taking a brief look at how the safeguards have worked to date, primarily focusing on some of the concerns raised by those who have personal experience of the safeguards (family, friends and 'P') as well as observations by professionals working in this area. The following has been written with the support of Mr and Mrs E who provided a valuable insight into the DoLS process based on their experience of others approaching them seeking guidance. It is also listed as a series of bullet points rather than explored in any detail by the author as at the time of writing we await the implementation of the Care Act as well as further guidance that may impact on these issues.

- Families report that they have not received either the Department of Health or other supplementary guidance about the safeguards, an explanation of the process or how they may deal with it.

- Family members report being excluded from the role of RPR despite the fact that the Department of Health make it clear that people should not be regarded as acting contrary to a person's best interests just because they object and/or are likely to challenge an authorization. There is currently no mechanism to challenge this.

- IMCAs are not being appointed as a matter of course to support an unpaid RPR, again despite Department of Health recommendations that there should be an automatic referral. Many RPRs are not even informed that they have a right to an IMCA.

- With regards best interests decisions, many report that there is minimal understanding given to the person's way of communicating or involving them in decision. Equally more time needs to be spent taking in the views of family, carers and other relevant people, past and present wishes and least restrictive alternatives.

- BIAs work in offices for the local authority that is also the supervisory body. This is not to suggest that professionals are not competent, but that consideration needs to be given to the fact that on one day a BIA (in their other role) is working with a colleague on one matter and then the next have their BIA hat on and may now be in conflict.

- Local Authorities change conditions from those set out in court orders without going back to the court for ratification. If family members are not the RPR then any challenge to LA is at vast expense.

Future resolution
But can the above be addressed, either in practice, training, resources, guidance or a change in the law? The DoL safeguards are crucial in protecting the rights and liberty of those that come

within its framework. If they are to work as intended, there must be clear consideration given to all elements of them, including where there is a risk that a gap occurs in their application. We therefore ask the reader to consider the following, some of which will in all likelihood be made clearer or addressed by current revision of the DoLS, but is still worth highlighting at this time.

- Residential contracts with local authorities to require managing authorities to demonstrate full training and appropriate qualifications for MCA and DoLS as a condition of placements.

- Local Authorities to be made accountable for inadequate implementation of Safeguards.

- Supported Living schemes specifically those run as pseudo residential homes to be brought into DoLS.

- More robust inspection by CQC and for registered providers to have a registered manager with inspectors, studying care plans and making judgments on DoL likelihood.

- Appointment of equivalent 39D IMCAs to support untrained, uninformed family members through the assessment process prior to authorization. Is 'appropriate to consult' (or rather 'inappropriate to consult') a criterion that needs to be re-examined to enable the instruction of an IMCA?

- BIAs to be independent by way of carrying out their role in other Local Authority areas.

- An appeal process for people who wish to challenge the appointment of RPR.

- Court orders to be followed up at an early stage and scrutinized; perhaps a role for the Official Solicitor or Court visitors or CQC.

- 39D IMCAs to be instructed as a matter of course, their appointment only to be terminated at the express wish of RPR.

At the time of writing we are expecting to see further guidance from the Department of Health and Law Commission.

References

Ashton, G. and Ward, A. (1992) *Mental Handicap and The Law*. London: Sweet and Maxwell.

Cowley, J. (2014) 'Why commissioning of mental capacity advocacy must change to protect rights of vulnerable.' *Community Care*. Available at: www.communitycare.co.uk/2014/02/04/commissioning-mental-capacity-advocacy-must-change-protect-rights-vulnerable, accessed on 2 December 2014.

Cowley, J. and Lee, S. (2010a) *IMCA Instruction: Best Practice Guidance*. Available at www.empowermentmatters.co.uk/Wordpress/wp-content/uploads/2012/07/IMCA-instruction-guidance2.pdf, accessed on 2 December 2014.

Cowley, J. and Lee, S. (2010b) *IMCA Report Writing: Best Practice Guidance*. Available at www.empowermentmatters.co.uk/Wordpress/wp-content/uploads/2012/07/IMCA-Report-Writing-Guidance.pdf, accessed on 2 December 2014.

Department of Health (2014) *The Sixth Year of the Independent Mental Capacity Advocacy Service (IMCA)*: 2012/2013. Available at www.gov.uk/dh, accessed on 2 December 2014.

Empowerment Matters (2012) Available at www.empowermentmatters.co.uk/Wordpress/wp-content/uploads/2012/07/A4A-SMT-best-practice-guidance1.pdf, accessed on 2 December 2014.

Ferns, P. (2012) 'Finding a Way Forward. A Black Perspective on Social Approaches to Mental Health.' In J. Tew. *Social Approaches in Mental Health*. London: Jessica Kingsley Publishers.

Francis, R. (2013). *The King's Fund Conference. Lessons From Stafford*. Available at www.kingsfund.org.uk/sites/files/kf/field/field_document/robert-francis-kingsfund-feb13.pdf, accessed on 3 February 2015.

GMC (2014) *Consent Guidance: Assessing Capacity*. Available at www.gmc-uk.org, accessed on 2 December 2014.

Ho, A. (2009) *Mental Capacity Act and DoLS Training Material*. Maidstone: Kent County Council.

Irwin Mitchell Solicitors. (2014) *Somerset County Council v MK Court of Protection Judgment*. Available at www.irwinmitchell.com, accessed on 2 December 2014.

Justice.gov.uk (2014) *Official Solicitor and Public Trustee*. Available at www.justice.gov.uk/about/ospt, accessed on 2 December 2014.

Jones, R. (2012) *Mental Capacity Act Manual*, 5th edn. London: Sweet and Maxwell.

Kent and Medway Local Implementation Network (2009) *Best Interests Checklist Document.* Maidstone: Kent County Council.

Kent and Medway Local Implementation Network (2009) Best Interests Meeting Agenda Document. Maidstone: Kent County Council.

Kramer (1995) 'Introduction' In Rogers, C. (1961). *On Becoming a Person.* New York: Houghton Mifflin Company.

Mental Capacity Act (2005). *Code of Practice.* London: The Stationery Office.

Ministry of Justice (2014) Mental Capacity Act: Making decisions https://www.gov.uk/government/collections/mental-capacity-act-making-decisions, accessed 3 February 2015.

NHS England (2012) *Compassion in Practice.* Available at www.england.nhs.uk, accessed on 2 December 2014.

NHS England (2012) www.england.nhs.uk, accessed on 2 December 2014.

SCIE (2014) *IMCA and Paid Relevant Person's Representative Roles in the Mental Capacity Act Deprivation of Liberty Safeguards.* Available at www.scie.org.uk/publications/guides/guide41/files/guide41.pdf, accessed on 2 December 2014.

SCIE (2013a) *Independent Mental Capacity Advocate Involvement in Accommodation Decisions and Care Reviews.* Available at www.scie.org.uk/publications/guides/guide39/files/guide39.pdf, accessed on 2 December 2014.

SCIE (2013b) *Practice guidance on the involvement of Independent Mental Capacity Advocates (IMCAs) in safeguarding adults.* Available at www.scie.org.uk/publications/guides/guide32/files/guide32.pdf, accessed on 2 December 2014.

Schön, D. (1983) *The Reflective Practitioner: How Professionals Think in Action.* New York: Basic Books.

Rogers, C. (1961) *On Becoming a Person.* New York: Houghton Mifflin Company.

The Mid Staffordshire NHS Foundation Trust Public Inquiry (chaired by Robert Francis QC) (2013) London: The Stationery Office.

Trevithick, P. (2012) *Social Work Skills and Knowledge. A Practice Handbook,* 3rd edn. Maidenhead: OU Press.

The Guardian (2012) *Winterbourne View care home staff jailed for abusing residents.* Available at www.theguardian.com/society/2012/oct/26/winterbourne-view-care-staff-jailed, accessed on 2 December 2014.

Thornicroft, G. *(2007)* Shunned: Discrimination against People with Mental Illness. Oxford: Oxford University Press.

Wolfensberger, W. and Zauha, H. (1973) *Citizen Advocacy and Protective Services for the Impaired and Handicapped.* Toronto: National Institute on Mental Retardation.

Index